VOGUE®
KNITTING
QUICK KNITS

VOGUE® KNITTING

QUICK KNITS

Edited by Trisha Malcolm

SIXTH&SPRING BOOKS
NEW YORK

SIXTH&SPRING BOOKS
233 Spring Street
New York, New York 10013

Editor-in-Chief
Trisha Malcolm

Editor
Michelle Lo

Art Director
Chi Ling Moy

Copy Editor
Jean Guirguis
Daryl Brower

Book Manager
Theresa McKeon

Yarn Editor
Veronica Manno

Contributors
Anne McNamara
Leslie Barber

Technical Editors
Carla Scott
Karen Greenwald

President and Publisher, Sixth&Spring Books
Art Joinnides

1 3 5 7 9 10 8 6 4 2

Library of Congress Cataloging-in-Publication Data
Vogue knitting quick knits/editor-in-chief Trisha Malcolm
p. cm.

ISBN:1-931543-07-0.Trade
ISBN: 1-931543-87-9 Paper
ISBN-13: 978-1-931543-87-3 Paper
1. Knitting—Patterns. I. Title: Quick knits. II. Malcolm, Trisha, 1960- III. Vogue knitting international
TT825.V637 2002
746.43'20432–dc21   2022022375

Manufactured in China

Introduction

Time flies. In 1982, *Vogue Knitting* magazine re-launched with a bi-annual publication of topnotch knitting patterns that put fashionable knitted garments within the reach of anyone who could wield two needles and a ball of yarn. On the pages were designs that ranged from simple to skilled—all of them sensational in their own right. The designs and their presentation appealed to a nation that was rediscovering the simple joys of making something by hand and carving out a little leisure time in what was becoming an increasingly fast-paced and frantic lifestyle. Twenty years and hundreds of patterns later, knitting is bigger than ever, even though the time we have to pursue our hobby is even more limited. That's where this book comes in.

When we began tossing around ideas for a new knitting title, we asked ourselves (and many others) what we, as knitters, needed. The resounding answer was "time." We all had great ideas and ambitions for new projects, but not enough hours in the day to accomplish them. So we dug into our magazine archives and pulled

out the quick-knitting designs that offered almost-instant gratification along with standout style. On these pages you'll find the results of our search—fun-to-knit projects that finish up fast without sacrificing style.

We also took the time to make sure you'd get great results. While many of the yarns used in the original designs are still available, others are no longer being manufactured or have had certain colors discontinued. Our technical and yarn editors spent hours stitching up swatches in search of a perfect substitute so that you will be pleased with the finished project. Whenever these substitutions have been made, we've also listed the original yarn—just in case you have a bag or two stashed away.

Our goal in pulling together this special collection was to offer a selection of patterns and projects that will inspire you to pick up your needles. From classic cardigans to trendy tank tops, there's something for every taste, age, skill level and season. Make time to peruse the pages, pick your project and get clicking. Trust us, you have the time—and the talent—to stitch up something truly fabulous.

Whether you're an old hand or a knitting newcomer, the patterns on these pages will put you on the fast track to knitting bliss.

Table of Contents

Before You Begin

This book was designed as an anthology of patterns. For more precise technical explanation, refer to Vogue Knitting—The Ultimate Knitting Book (New York: Sixth&Spring Books).

YARN SELECTION

Some of the yarns, or colors, used in the original patterns are no longer available. We have provided substitute yarns readily available in the U.S. and Canada at the time of printing. The Resources on page 158 lists addresses of yarn distributors—contact them for the name of a retailer in your area or for mail-order information.

If you wish to substitute a yarn, check the gauge carefully to ensure the finished garment will knit to the correct measurements. To facilitate yarn substitution, Vogue Knitting grades yarn by the standard stitch gauge obtained in stockinette stitch. There is a grading number in the Materials section of each pattern. Look for a substitute yarn that falls into the same category—the suggested gauge on the ball band should be comparable to that on the Yarn Symbols Chart (right).

After successfully gauge-swatching in a substitute yarn, you'll need to determine yarn requirements. First, find the total length of the original yarn in the pattern (multiply number of balls by yards/meters per ball). Divide this figure by the new yards/meters per ball (listed on the ball band). Round up to the next whole number. The answer is the number of balls required.

GAUGE

To ensure a successful project, always knit a gauge swatch before beginning. Normally, gauge is measured over a four-inch (10cm) square. Using the needles and yarn suggested, cast on enough stitches to knit a square at least this size. Gauge is usually given in stockinette stitch, but if the pattern calls for a specific stitch, work this stitch for the swatch. Measure stitches carefully with a ruler or gauge tool. If the swatch is smaller than the stated gauge (more stitches per inch/cm), try larger needles. If it is larger (fewer stitches per inch/cm), use smaller needles. Before proceeding, experiment with needle size until the gauge exactly matches the one given.

If a pattern calls for knitting in the round, it may tighten the gauge, so if the gauge was measured on a flat swatch, take another reading after beginning the project.

READING PATTERNS

Each pattern is rated for technical ability.

YARN SYMBOLS

The following numbers 1-6 represent a range of stitch gauges. Note that these numbers correspond to the standard gauge in stockinette stitch.

1 FINE WEIGHT
(29-32 stitches per 4"/10cm)
Includes baby and fingering yarns, and some of the heavier crochet cottons.

2 LIGHTWEIGHT
(25-28 stitches per 4"/10cm)
Includes sport yarn, sock yarn, UK 4-ply and lightweight DK yarns.

3 MEDIUM WEIGHT
(21-24 stitches per 4"/10cm)
Includes DK and worsted, the most commonly used knitting yarns.

4 MEDIUM-HEAVY WEIGHT
(17-20 stitches per 4"/10cm)
Also called heavy worsted or Aran.

5 BULKY WEIGHT
(13-16 stitches per 4"/10cm)
Also called chunky. Includes heavier Icelandic yarns.

6 EXTRA-BULKY WEIGHT
(9-12 stitches per 4"/10cm)
The heaviest yarns available.

Choose a pattern that fits within your experience range. Read all instructions thoroughly before starting to knit a gauge swatch and again before beginning a project. Familiarize yourself with all abbreviations (see Knitting Terms and Abbreviations, opposite). Refer to the *Vogue Knitting* book for clear explanations of any stitches or techniques you may not be familiar with.

Generally, patterns are written in several sizes. The smallest appears first, and figures for larger sizes are given in parentheses. Where only one figure appears, it applies to all sizes. Highlight numbers pertaining to your size before beginning.

Knitted measurements are the dimensions of the garment after all the pieces have been sewn together. Usually, three measurements are given: finished chest; finished length; and sleeve width at upper arm. The finished chest measurement is the width around the entire sweater at the underarm. For cardigans, the width is determined with the front bands buttoned. Finished length is measured from the highest point of the shoulder to the bottom of the ribbing. Sleeve width is measured at the upper arm, after all increases have been worked and before any cap shaping takes place.

Schematics are a valuable tool for determining size selection and proper fit. Schematics are scale drawings showing the dimensions of the finished knitted pieces.

Work figures given inside brackets the number of times stated afterward. Directions immediately following an asterisk are to be repeated the given number of times. If the instructions call for working even, work in the same pattern stitch without increasing or decreasing.

KNITTING TERMS AND ABBREVIATIONS

approx approximately

beg begin(ning)

bind off Used to finish an edge and keep stitches from unraveling. Lift the first stitch over the second, the second over the third, etc. (UK: cast off)

cast on A foundation row of stitches placed on the needle in order to begin knitting.

CC contrast color

ch chain(s)

cm centimeter(s)

cont continue(ing)

dc double crochet (UK: tr-treble)

dec decrease(ing)—Reduce the stitches in a row (knit 2 together).

dpn double-pointed needle(s)

foll follow(s)(ing)

g gram(s)

garter stitch Knit every row. Circular knitting: knit one round, then purl one round.

hdc half-double crochet (UK: htr-half treble)

inc increase(ing)—Add stitches in a row (knit into the front and back of a stitch).

k knit

k2tog knit 2 stitches together

lp(s) loops(s)

LH left hand

m meter(s)

M1 make one stitch—With the needle tip, lift the strand between the last stitch worked and next stitch on the left-hand needle and knit into the back of it. One stitch has been added.

MC main color

mm millimeter(s)

oz ounce(s)

p purl

p2tog purl 2 stitches together

pat pattern

pick up and knit (purl) Knit (or purl) into the loops along an edge.

pm place markers—Place or attach a loop of contrast yarn or purchased stitch marker as indicated.

psso pass slip stitch over

rem remain(s)(ing)

rep repeat

rev St st reverse Stockinette stitch—Purl right-side rows, knit wrong-side rows. Circular knitting: purl all rounds. (UK: reverse stocking stitch)

rnd(s) round(s)

RH right hand

RS right side(s)

sc single crochet (UK: dc - double crochet)

sk skip

SKP Slip 1, knit 1, pass slip stitch over knit 1

sl slip—An unworked stitch made by passing a stitch from the left-hand to the right-hand needle as if to purl.

sl st slip stitch (UK: single crochet)

ssk slip, slip, knit—Slip next 2 stitches knitwise, one at a time, to right-hand needle. Insert tip of left-hand needle into fronts of these stitches from left to right. Knit them together. One stitch has been decreased.

st(s) stitch(es)

St st Stockinette stitch—Knit right-side rows, purl wrong-side rows. Circular knitting: knit all rounds. (UK: stocking stitch)

tbl through back of loop

tog together

WS wrong side(s)

wyif with yarn in front

wyib with yarn in back

work even Continue in pattern without increasing or decreasing. (UK: work straight)

yd yard(s)

yo yarn over—Make a new stitch by wrapping the yarn over the right-hand needle. (UK: yfwd, yon, yrn)

* repeat directions following * as many times as indicated.

[ ] Repeat directions inside brackets as many times as indicated.

FOLLOWING CHARTS

Charts are a convenient way to follow colorwork, lace, cable, and other stitch patterns. *Vogue Knitting* stitch charts utilize the universal language of "symbolcraft." Each symbolcraft symbol represents the stitch as it appears on the right side of the work. For example, the symbol for the knit stitch is a vertical line and the symbol for a purl stitch is a horizontal one. On right-side rows, work the stitches as they appear on the chart—knitting the vertical lines and purling the horizontal ones. When reading wrong-side rows, work the opposite of what is shown; that is, purl the vertical lines and knit the horizontal ones.

Each square on a chart represents one stitch and each horizontal row of squares equals a row or round. When knitting back and forth on straight needles, right-side rows (RS) are read right to left, wrong-side rows (WS) are read from left to right, bottom to top. When knitting in rounds on circular needles, read charts from right to left on every round, repeating any stitch and row repeats as directed in the pattern. Posting a self-adhesive note under the working row is an easy way to keep track on a chart.

Sometimes, only a single repeat of the pattern is charted. Heavy lines drawn through the entire chart indicate a repeat. The lines are the equivalent of an asterisk (*) or brackets [] used in written instructions.

KNITTING NEEDLES		
US	**METRIC**	**UK**
0	2mm	14
1	2.25mm	13
	2.5mm	
2	2.75mm	12
	3mm	11
3	3.25mm	10
4	3.5mm	
5	3.75mm	9
	4mm	8
6		
7	4.5mm	7
8	5mm	6
9	5mm	5
10	6mm	4
10½	6.5mm	3
	7mm	2
	7.5mm	1
11	8mm	0
13	9mm	00
15	10mm	000

Cool and Casual

Lighten up!
The new knits of spring
have grace
and sophistication
making warm-weather
dressing a breeze.

Clean, crisp and thoroughly modern, white always makes a high-impact statement. Simple ribbed stitching accents a sleek silhouette creating a sure-to-be summer classic. Shown in size Medium/Large. Designed by Kristen Nicholas, the Boatneck Pullover first appeared in the Spring/Summer '01 issue of *Vogue Knitting*.

Boatneck Pullover

VERY EASY VERY VOGUE

SIZES
To fit Small, Medium/Large. Directions are for smallest size with larger sizes in parentheses. If there is only one figure, it applies to all sizes.

KNITTED MEASUREMENTS
● Bust 43 (51)"/109 (129.5)cm
● Length 22½ (23)"/57 (58.5)cm
● Upper arm 20 (21½)"/51 (54.5)cm

MATERIALS
● 13 (13) 3½oz/100g hanks (each approx 51yd/47m) of Classic Elite Yarns *Weekend-Cotton* (cotton 5) in #4801 white
● One pair size 15 (10mm) needles OR SIZE TO OBTAIN GAUGE

GAUGE
9 sts and 14 rows = 4"/10cm over rib pat st using size 15 (10mm) needles. FOR PERFECT FIT, TAKE TIME TO CHECK GAUGE.

RIB PATTERN STITCH
(multiple of 9 sts plus 3)
Row 1 (WS) K1, p1, k1, *p1, k4, p1, k1, p1, k1; rep from * to end.
Row 2 (RS) *P1, k1 tbl, p1, k1 tbl, p4, k1 tbl; rep from *, end p1, k1 tbl, p1.
Rep these 2 rows for rib pat st.

BACK
Cast on 48 (57) sts. Work in rib pat st until piece measures 22½ (23)"/57 (58.5)cm from beg. Bind off in rib. Place markers at 13 (17) sts from each side seam at top to indicate end of shoulders.

FRONT
Work as for back.

SLEEVES
Cast on 21 sts. Work in rib pat st for 1½"/4cm. Inc 1 st each side (working inc sts in rib pat) on next row, then every 4th row 12 (13) times more— 47 (49) sts. Work even until piece measures 17"/43cm from beg. Bind off in rib.

FINISHING
Block pieces to measurements. Sew shoulder seams to markers, leaving 10"/25.5cm open for neck. Place markers at 10 (10¾)"/25.5 (27)cm down from shoulders. Sew top of sleeves to armholes between markers. Sew side and sleeve seams.

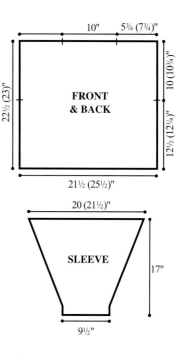

Joan Vass's easy-to-knit pullover—highlighted by a compelling openwork pattern, drop shoulders and ribbed finishing—is a breath of fresh air. This exquisite stunner leaves little to be desired. Shown in size Small. The Rolled-Neck Openwork Top first appeared in the Spring/Summer '99 issue of *Vogue Knitting*.

Rolled-Neck Openwork Top

VERY EASY VERY VOGUE

SIZES
To fit Small (Medium, Large, X-Large). Directions are for smallest size with larger size in parentheses. If there is only one figure, it applies to all sizes.

KNITTED MEASUREMENTS
● Bust 41 (44, 47, 49)"/104 (111.5, 119, 124.5)cm
● Length 19 (19, 19½, 20)"/48 (48, 49.5, 50.5)cm
● Upper arm 11½ (11½, 12½, 14)"/29 (29, 32, 35.5)cm

MATERIALS
● 9 (9, 10, 11) 1¾oz/50g skeins (each approx 99yd/90m) of Trendsetter Yarns *Dolcino* (acrylic /polyamide 5) in #8 moss green
● One pair each sizes 9 and 11 (5.5 and 8mm) needles OR SIZE TO OBTAIN GAUGE
● Size 9 (5.5mm) circular needle, 16"/40cm long
● Size I/9 (5.5mm) crochet hook

GAUGE
12 sts and 21 rows = 4"/10cm over openwork pat st using larger needles. FOR PERFECT FIT, TAKE TIME TO CHECK GAUGE.

Note
Body is made in one piece, beg at lower back and worked to neck, then sts are bound off for back neck then cast on for front neck and front is worked to lower edge.

OPENWORK PATTERN STITCH
(multiple of 4 sts plus 2 selvage sts).
Row 1 (RS) K1 (selvage st), *k2, yo twice, k2; rep from *, end k1 (selvage st).
Row 2 K1, *p2tog, work k1, p1 into double yo, p2tog; rep from *, end k1.
Row 3 K1, *yo, k4, yo; rep from *, end k1.
Row 4 K1, *p1, p2tog twice, k1; rep from *, end k1.
Rep rows 1-4 for openwork pat st.

BODY
Beg at lower edge with smaller needles, cast on 59 (63, 67, 71) sts. Work in k1, p1 rib for 1¼"/3cm, inc 3 sts evenly on last WS row—62 (66, 70, 74) sts. Change to larger needles and cont in openwork pat st until piece measures 19 (19, 19½, 20)"/48 (48, 49.5, 50.5)cm from beg. **Next row (RS)** Work 19 (21, 23, 25) sts, bind off 24 sts for neck, work to end. **Next row (WS)** Work in pat casting on 24 sts over bound-off sts of previous row. Cont in pat st on all sts until piece measures 17¾ (17¾, 18¼, 18¾)"/45 (45, 46.5, 47.5)cm from front neck (same number of rows as back to ribbed edge). Change to smaller needles and k1, p1 rib, dec 3 sts on next row and cont in k1, p1 rib for 1¼"/3cm. Bind off in rib.

SLEEVES
With smaller needles, cast on 33 (33, 35, 39) sts. Work in k1, p1 rib for 1¼"/3cm inc 1 (1, 3, 3) sts on last WS row—34 (34, 38, 42) sts. Change to larger needle and work in openwork pat st until piece measures 16½"/42cm from beg. Bind off loosely in pat.

FINISHING
Do not steam block pieces. Pin pieces to measurements and mist lightly and allow to dry.

Neckband
With circular needle, pick up and k 60 sts evenly around neck. Work in St st (k every rnd) for 2"/5cm. Bind off. Foll neckband to outside. Place markers at 6 (6, 6½, 7¼)"/15 (15, 16.5, 18.5)cm down from shoulders. With crochet hook, sl st sleeves to armhole between markers from WS. Sl st side seams and sleeve seams tog from WS.

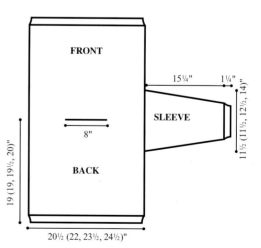

When mercury rises, keep your cool in Viola Carol's variegated poolside cover-up. Make this easy ribbed number, and a matching one for your pooch, over a long lazy weekend. Shown in size Medium. The Twisted Rib Pullover first appeared in the Spring/Summer '01 issue of *Vogue Knitting*.

Twisted Rib Pullover

VERY EASY VERY VOGUE

SIZES
To fit Small, Medium, Large. Directions are for smallest size with larger sizes in parentheses. If there is only one figure, it applies to all sizes.

KNITTED MEASUREMENTS
● Bust 35 (37, 39½)"/89 (94, 100)cm
● Length 19 (19½, 20)"/48 (49.5, 50.5)cm
● Upper arm 11 (11¾, 12½)"/28 (30, 32)cm

MATERIALS
● 7 (8, 9) 1¾oz/50g balls (each approx 107yd/100m) of Brown Sheep Co. *Kaleidoscope* (cotton/wool 4) in #10 Belize
● One pair size 9 (5.5mm) needles OR SIZE TO OBTAIN GAUGE
● 1yd/1m of ¼"/6mm leather lacing

Dog Sweater
● 1 ball in #10 Belize
● One pair size 10½ (6.5mm) needles OR SIZE TO OBTAIN GAUGE
● Size J (6mm) crochet hook

GAUGE
18 sts and 19 rows = 4"/10cm over twisted rib pat using size 9 (5.5mm) needles. FOR PERFECT FIT, TAKE TIME TO CHECK GAUGE.

TWISTED RIB
(odd number of sts)
Row 1 (RS) K1 tbl, *p1, k1 tbl; rep from * to end.
Row 2 P1, *k1 tbl, p1; rep from * to end.
Rep these 2 rows for twisted rib.

BACK
Cast on 73 (77, 83) sts. Work in twisted rib for 4½"/11.5cm. Inc 1 st each side of next row then every 10th row twice more—79 (83, 89) sts. Work even until piece measures 11½"/29cm from beg.

Armhole shaping
Bind off 5 sts at beg of next 2 rows. Dec 1 st each side every other row 1 (2, 4) times—67 (69, 71) sts. Work even until armhole measures 7½ (8, 8½)"/19 (20.5, 21.5)cm. Bind off all sts knitwise.

FRONT
Work as for back until piece measures 9½"/24cm from beg. Mark center st of row.

Divide for neck
Next row (RS) Work to 2 sts before center st, k2tog, join another ball of yarn and bind off center st, SKP, work to end. Cont to work both sides at once, work to armhole. Then work armhole shaping as on back—32 (33, 34) sts rem each side. Work even until armhole measures 6½ (7, 7½)"/16.5 (18, 19)cm.

Neck shaping
Bind off 13 (13, 14) sts from each neck edge and work each side separately until same length as back. Bind off rem 19 (20, 20) sts each side for shoulders.

SLEEVES
Cast on 41 (43, 43) sts. Work in twisted rib for 4"/10cm. Inc 1 st each side of next row and rep inc every 12th (10th, 8th) row 3 (4, 6) times more—49 (53, 57) sts. Work even until piece measures 17½"/44.5cm from beg.

Cap shaping
Bind off 5 sts at beg of next 2 rows. Dec 1 st each side of every other row 8 (9, 10) times. Bind off 2 sts at beg of next 2 rows, 2 (2, 3) sts at beg of next 2 rows. Bind off rem 15 (17, 17) sts.

FINISHING
Block pieces to measurements. Sew shoulder seams. Sew sleeves into armholes. Sew side and sleeve seams. Thread lacing through center front opening as in photo.

DOG SWEATER

GAUGE
12 sts and 18 rows = 4"/10cm over twisted St st using a double strand of yarn and size 10½/ 6.5mm needles. TAKE TIME TO CHECK GAUGE.

SWEATER

Beg at lower edge with double strand of yarn, cast on 40 sts. **Row 1 (RS)** *K1 tbl, p1; rep from * to end. Rep row 1 for twisted rib for 2"/5cm. **Next row (RS)** *K1 tbl; rep from * across. **Next row (WS)** Purl. Rep these 2 rows for twisted St st inc 1 st each side every other row 4 times, AT SAME TIME, when piece measures 3½"/9cm from beg, work as foll:

Leg openings

Next row (RS) Work 6 sts, join another 2 balls of yarn and bind off 4 sts, work to last 10 sts, join another 2 balls of yarn and bind off 4 sts, work 6 sts. Work each section with separate balls of yarn for 3 rows. **Next row** Cast on 4 sts over each set of bound-off sts to rejoin piece. Work even for 5 rows more on 48 sts. Bind off 4 sts at beg of next 2 rows. Dec 1 st each side every 4th row 3 times. Bind off 5 sts at beg of next 4 rows. Bind off rem 14 sts.

FINISHING

Block piece lightly. Pick up and k 64 sts evenly along entire shaped top edge, beg with 4-st bind-offs. Work in k1, p1 rib for 2 rows. Bind off. Sew sides of rows tog for under seams.

Straps (2)

With crochet hook and double strand of yarn, ch 24. Sew straps to inside to secure around front legs.

WOMEN'S SWEATER

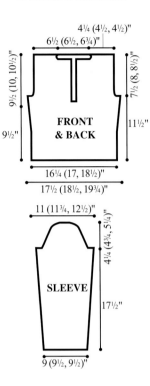

Garter-Stitch Cardigan Set

Beat the summer heat with this winning pair in cool, comfortable cotton. Viola Carol's take on the twin set pairs a flirty garter-stitch cardigan with a slim ribbed tank. Shown in size Small. The Garter-Stitch Cardigan Set first appeared in the Spring/Summer '01 issue of *Vogue Knitting*.

Garter-Stitch Cardigan Set

VERY EASY VERY VOGUE

SIZES
To fit Small, Medium, Large. Directions are for smallest size with larger sizes in parentheses. If there is only one figure, it applies to all sizes.

KNITTED MEASUREMENTS
Cardigan
● Bust 35½ (37½, 40)"/90 (95, 101.5)cm
● Length 20½ (21, 21½)"/52 (53.5, 54.5)cm
● Upper arm 13 (14¼, 15½)"/33 (36, 39.5)cm
Tank top
● Bust 32 (34, 36)"/81 (86, 91.5)cm
● Length 17½ (18, 18¼)"/44.5 (45.5, 46.5)cm

MATERIALS
Cardigan
● 11 (12, 13) 1¾oz/50g skeins (each approx 70yd/64m) of Classic Elite Yarns *Newport* (cotton 4) in #2001 white (A)
Tank top
● 6 (7, 7) hanks in #2016 natural (B)
● One pair each sizes 10 and 10½ (6 and 6.5mm) needles OR SIZE TO OBTAIN GAUGE
● Size J/10 (6mm) crochet hook

GAUGE
14 sts and 26 rows = 4"/10cm over garter st using size 10½ (6.5mm) needles.
16 sts and 19 rows = 4"/10cm over k1, p1 twisted rib using size 10 (6mm) needles.
FOR PERFECT FIT, TAKE TIME TO CHECK GAUGES.

CARDIGAN

BACK
With larger needles and A, cast on 62 (66, 70) sts. Work in garter st until piece measures 13"/33cm from beg.

Armhole shaping
Bind off 5 sts at beg of next 2 rows. Dec 1 st each side every other row 0 (1, 1) time—52 (54, 58) sts. Work even until armhole measures 7½ (8, 8½)"/19 (20.5, 21.5)cm. Bind off all sts.

LEFT FRONT
With larger needles and A, cast on 35 (37, 39) sts. Work in garter st until piece measures 13"/33cm from beg.

Armhole shaping
Bind off 5 sts at beg of next RS row (armhole edge), then dec 1 st at armhole edge every other row 0 (1, 1) time—30 (31, 33) sts. Work even until armhole measures 5½ (6, 6½)"/14 (15, 16.5)cm.

Neck shaping
Next row (WS) Bind off 10 (11, 11) sts, work to end. Cont to dec 1 st at neck edge every row 5 times—15 (15, 17) sts. When same length as back, bind off rem sts for shoulder.

RIGHT FRONT
Work to correspond to left front, reversing shaping.

SLEEVES
With larger needles and A, cast on 40 (44, 48) sts. Work in garter st, inc 1 st each side every 14th row 3 times—46 (50, 54) sts. Work even until piece measures 10"/25.5cm from beg.

Cap shaping
Bind off 5 sts at beg of next 2 rows. Dec 1 st each side every other row 14 (16, 18) times. Bind off rem 8 sts.

FINISHING
Block pieces lightly to measurements. Sew shoulder seams. Sew sleeves into armholes. Sew side and sleeve seams. With crochet hook and 2 strands B, chain 10"/25.5cm for each tie and fasten securely at top of neck.

TANK TOP

BACK
With smaller needles and B, cast on 59 (63, 67) sts. Twisted rib—**Row 1 (RS)** *K1 tbl, p1; rep from *, end k1 tbl. Row 2 P1 tbl, *k1, p1 tbl; rep from * to end. Rep these 2 rows for twisted rib, inc 1 st each side, working inc sts into rib, every 12th row 3 times—65 (69, 73) sts. Work even until piece measures 11½"/29cm from beg.

Armhole shaping
Bind off 7 (8, 8) sts at beg of next 2 rows—51 (53, 57) sts. Work even until armhole measures 2½ (3, 3¼)"/6.5 (7.5, 8)cm.

Neck shaping
Work 12 sts, join 2nd ball of yarn and bind off center 27 (29, 33) sts in rib, work to end. Work on 12 sts each side for straps until armhole measures 6 (6½, 6¾)"/15 (16.5, 17)cm with straps slightly stretched. Bind off.

FRONT

Work as for back until armholes measure 2 (2½, 2¾)"/5 (6.5, 7)cm.

Neck shaping

Work as for back neck shaping, then work straps to same length as back.

FINISHING

Block pieces lightly to measurements. Sew side and shoulder seams.

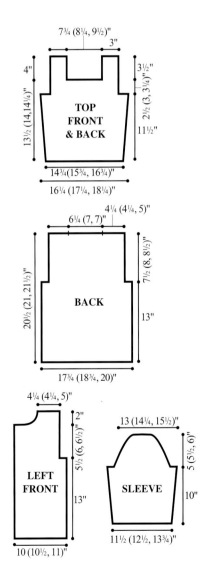

TOP FRONT & BACK

7¾ (8¼, 9½)"
3"
4"
3½"
13½ (14,14¼)"
2½ (3, 3¼)"
11½"
14¾(15¾, 16¾)"
16¼ (17¼, 18¼)"

BACK

4¼ (4¼, 5)"
6¼ (7, 7)"
7½ (8, 8½)"
20½ (21, 21½)"
13"
17¾ (18¾, 20)"

LEFT FRONT

4¼ (4¼, 5)"
2"
5½ (6, 6½)"
13"
10 (10½, 11)"

SLEEVE

13 (14¼, 15½)"
5 (5½, 6)"
10"
11½ (12½, 13¾)"

Light and lacy, this exquisite little tunic gives the illusion of transparency without baring all. A ribbed neck and crochet trim lend an air of easy elegance. Designed by Mari Lynn Patrick. Shown in Medium. The Openwork Pullover first appeared in the Spring/Summer '98 issue of *Vogue Knitting*.

Openwork Pullover

VERY EASY VERY VOGUE

SIZES
To fit X-Small (Small, Medium, Large, X-Large). Directions are for smallest size with larger sizes in parentheses. If there is only one figure it applies to all sizes.

KNITTED MEASUREMENTS
● Bust 35 (37, 40, 42, 44½)"/89 (94, 101.5, 106.5, 113) cm
● Lower edge 47 (49, 51, 54, 56)"/119 (124.5, 129.5, 137, 142)cm
● Length 25¾ (26¼, 27, 27½, 28¼)"/65.5 (67, 68.5,70,71.5)cm
● Upper arm 15½ (15½, 16½, 16½, 17½)"/39.5 (39.5, 42, 42, 44.5)cm

MATERIALS
● 5 (5, 5, 6, 6) 3½oz/100g skeins (each approx 216yd/200m) of Colinette/Unique Kolours *Framework Chenille* Cotton DK (cotton 4) in 18 gold
● One pair each sizes 9 and 10½ (5.5 and 7mm) needles OR SIZE TO OBTAIN GAUGE
● Size 7 (4.5mm) circular needle, 24"/60cm long
● Size G/6 (4.5mm) crochet hook

GAUGE
14 sts and 22 rows = 4"/10cm over pat st using smaller needles.
FOR PERFECT FIT, TAKE TIME TO CHECK GAUGE.

PATTERN STITCH
(multiple of 4 sts plus 2 selvage sts)
Row 1 (RS) K1 (selvage st), *k2, yo twice, k2; rep from *, end k1 (selvage st).
Row 2 K1, *p2tog, work k1, p1 in double yo, p2tog; rep from *, end k1.
Row 3 K1, *yo, k4, yo; rep from *, end k1.
Row 4 K1, *p1, p2tog twice, k1; rep from *, end k1. Rep rows 1-4 for pat st.
Note Decs for side seams alternate between k3tog, first at beg of row, then at another interval, k3tog at end of row.

BACK
With larger needle, cast on very loosely, 82 (86, 90, 94, 98) sts. Change to smaller needles and work in pat st for 2"/5cm. *Next row (RS) K3tog, (dec 2) work pat to end. Cont in pat as established for 7 rows more. **Next row (RS)** Work pat to last 3 sts, k3tog. Cont in pat st for 7 rows more*. Rep between *'s 4 times more—62 (66, 70, 74, 78) sts. Work even until piece measures 17 (17½, 18, 18, 18)"/43 (44.5, 45.5, 45.5, 45.5)cm from beg, end with a WS row.

Raglan armhole shaping
Next (dec) row (RS) K3tog, work pat to last 3 sts, k3tog. *Rep dec row every 2nd row once, every 4th row once*. Rep between *'s 0 (2, 3, 3, 4) times more. Rep dec row every 4th (4th, 2nd, 2nd, 4th) row 5 (2, 1, 2, 1) times. Work 1 (1, 3, 3, 1) rows even. Bind off rem 30 sts.

FRONT
Work same as back.

SLEEVES
With larger needle, cast on very loosely 30 (30, 34, 34, 38) sts. Change to smaller needles and work in pat st for 6 rows. *Next row (RS) K 1 in back, front and back of st (inc 2), work pat to end. Cont in pat as established for 5 rows more. **Next row (RS)** Work pat to last st, inc 2 sts in last st. Cont in pat st for 5 rows more *. Rep between *'s 5 times more—54 (54, 58, 58, 62) sts. Work even in pat st until piece measures 17"/43cm from beg.

Cap shaping
Next (dec) row (RS) K3tog, pat to last 3 sts, k3tog. Rep dec row every 4th row 6 (6, 7, 7, 8) times more. Work 3 (3, 1, 3, 3) rows even. Bind off rem 26 sts.

FINISHING
Block pieces to measurements. Sew raglan seams.

Neckband
With RS facing, circular needle and working into back lps only of bound-off sts, *pick up and k 1 st in one corner, (mark corner), 30 sts across front, 2 sts in corner (mark corner), 28 sts across sleeve, 2 sts in corner, (mark corner), 30 sts across back, 2 sts in corner (mark corner), 28 sts across sleeve, 1 st in corner—124 sts. Rnd 1 *Ssk, [p2, k2] 7

times, k2tog, ssk, [p2, k2] 6 times, p2, k2tog; rep from * once. Rnd 2 Work even in rib as established. Rnd 3 Ssk, *rib to 1 st before 2 corner sts, k2tog, ssk; rep from * 3 times, ending last rep k2tog. Rep rnds 2 and 3 twice more. Rep rnd 3 once. Bind off in rib. Sew side and sleeve seams.

Crochet edge

With RS facing and crochet hook, work 1 rnd of sc evenly around lower edge and sleeve cuff edges. Ch 1, do not turn, work 1 hdc in back lps only of each sc. Fasten off.

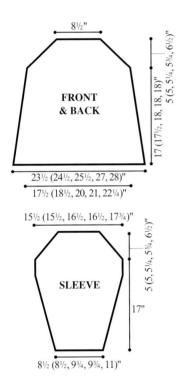

8½"

FRONT
& BACK

17 (17½, 18, 18, 18)"
5 (5, 5¼, 5¾, 6½)"

23½ (24½, 25½, 27, 28)"
17½ (18½, 20, 21, 22¼)"

15½ (15½, 16½, 16½, 17¾)"

SLEEVE

5 (5, 5¼, 5¾, 6½)"

17"

8½ (8½, 9¾, 9¾, 11)"

Stripe it rich with this simple shell and cardigan set by Susan Mills. Perfect for warmer weather, the cardigan features ribbed edging, set-in sleeves and simple shaping. Paired with the coordinating solid shell, it's a timeless classic. Shown in size Small. The Striped Twin Set first appeared in the Spring/Summer '00 issue of *Vogue Knitting*.

Striped Twin Set

VERY EASY VERY VOGUE

SIZES
To fit Small (Medium, Large). Directions are for smallest size with larger sizes in parentheses. If there is only one figure, it applies to all sizes.

KNITTED MEASUREMENTS
Cardigan
● Bust 36 (38, 40)"/91.5 (96.5, 101.5)cm
● Length 22 (22½, 23)"/56 (57, 58.5)cm
● Upper arm 15 (16, 17)"/38 (40.5, 43)cm

Top
● Bust 33 (35, 37)"/83.5 (89, 94)cm
● Length 22 (22¼, 22½)"/56 (56.5, 57)cm

MATERIALS
● 3 (4, 4) 1¾oz/50g balls (each approx 109yd/100m) of Reynolds/JCA *Tiara* (cotton/linen 4) in #13 mineral (A)
● 3 (3, 3) 1¾oz/50g balls (each approx 109yd/102m) of *Madrid* (cotton/linen 3) in #21 green (B)
● 3 (3, 3) 1¾oz/50g balls (each approx 110yd/101m) of *Cantata* (cotton/nylon 4) in #204 pale blue (C)
● 3 1¾oz/50g balls (each approx 101yd/93m) of *Serenity* (cotton 4) in #905 green (D)
● 3 (4, 4) 1¾oz/50g balls (each approx 78yd/60m) of *Meadow* (cotton/viscose/ linen 4) in #127 blue (E)
● One pair size 5 (3.75mm) needles OR SIZE TO OBTAIN GAUGE
● One each size 6 and 7 (4 and 4.5mm) circular needles, 36"/92cm long
● Five ⅝"/15mm buttons

GAUGE
● 19 sts and 26 rows = 4"/10cm over St st and stripe pat for cardigan using A-E and size 7 (4.5mm) needles.
● 21 sts and 28 rows = 4"/10cm over St st for top using A and size 5 (3.75mm) needles.
FOR PERFECT FIT, TAKE TIME TO CHECK GAUGES.

Note
Body of cardigan is knit in one piece on a circular needle.

STRIPE PATTERN
Work 2 rows B, 2 rows C, 4 rows D, 6 rows E, 2 rows A, 2 rows B, 4 rows C, 6 rows D, 2 rows E, 2 rows A, 4 rows B, 6 rows C, 2 rows D, 2 rows E, 4 rows A, 6 rows B, 2 rows C, 2 rows D, 4 rows E, 6 rows A. Rep these 70 rows for stripe pat.

CARDIGAN

BODY
With smaller circular needle and A, cast on 164 (172, 184) sts. **Row 1 (RS)** K3, *p2, k2; rep from *, end k1. Row 2 P3, *k2, p2; rep from * end p1. Rep rows 1 and 2 for k2, p2 rib for 1½"/4cm, inc 0 (2, 2) sts on last WS row—164 (174, 186) sts. Change to larger circular needle and cont in stripe pat until piece measures 13½"/34cm from beg. Divide for fronts and back.
Next row (RS) Work 37 (39, 43) sts and leave unworked for right front, bind off 8 sts for armhole, work 74 (80, 84) sts for back, leave rem 45 (47, 51) sts unworked. Working on sts for back only, shape armholes as foll: P 1 row. Dec

row (RS) K1, ssk, k to last 3 sts, k2tog, k1. Rep dec row every other row 3 times more—66 (72, 76) sts. Work even until armhole measures 7½ (8, 8½)"/19 (20.5, 21.5)cm.

Neck and shoulder shaping
Bind off 5 (6, 7) sts at beg of next 4 rows, 5 (6, 6) sts at beg of next 2 rows, AT SAME TIME, bind off center 32 sts and working both sides at once, dec 1 st from each neck edge every other row twice.

RIGHT FRONT
Return to first 37 (39, 43) sts and shape armhole as for back—33 (35, 39) sts. Work even until armhole measures 5½ (6, 6½)"/14 (15, 16.5)cm.

Neck shaping
Next row (RS) Bind off 5 (5, 6) sts, k to end. Cont to bind off 3 sts from neck edge every other row 3 (2, 3) times, 2 sts 1 (2, 1) times, 1 st twice—15 (18, 20) sts. When same length as back, shape shoulder as for back.

LEFT FRONT
Rejoin yarn to rem sts and bind off 8 sts for armhole, work to end. Work to correspond to right front, reversing shaping.

SLEEVES
With size 6 (4mm) needle and A, cast on 38 sts. Work in k2, p2 rib for 1½"/4cm. Change to size 7 (4.5mm) needle and cont in stripe pat, inc 1 st every 4th row 5 (9, 12) times, every 6th row 12 (10, 9) times—72 (76, 80) sts. Work even until piece measures 17½"/44.5cm from beg.

Cap shaping
Bind off 2 sts at beg of next 8 rows. Bind off rem 56 (60, 64) sts.

FINISHING
Block pieces to measurements. Sew shoulder seams. With smaller circular needle and A, pick up and k 96 (94, 98) sts evenly around neck edge. Work in k2, p2 rib for 1½"/4cm. Bind off in rib.

Left front band
With smaller circular needle and A, pick up and k 98 (100, 102) sts evenly along left front. Work in k2, p2 rib for 1½"/4cm. Bind off in rib. Place markers at ½"/1cm from top and lower edges on band for buttons and 3 more markers evenly spaced between. Work right front band to correspond, working a buttonhole opposite markers on 4th row by binding off 2 sts for each buttonhole then casting on 2 sts over each buttonhole on next row. Sew sleeves into armholes. Sew side and sleeve seams. Sew on buttons.

TOP

BACK
With size 5 (3.75mm) needles and A, cast on 86 (92, 98) sts. Work in k2, p2 rib for 1½"/4cm. Then cont in St st until piece measures 13"/33cm from beg.

Armhole shaping
Bind off 5 (5, 6) sts at beg of next 2 rows, 2 sts at beg of next 2 rows. Dec 1 st each side every other row 7 (9, 10) times—58 (60, 62) sts. Work even until armhole measures 7 (7¼, 7½)"/17.5 (18.5, 19)cm.

Neck and shoulder shaping
Next row (RS) K15 (16, 17) sts, join 2nd ball of yarn and bind off center 28 sts, work to end. Working both sides at once, dec 1 st at each neck edge every other row 3 times, AT SAME TIME, when armhole measures 8 (8¼, 8½)"/20 (21, 21.5)cm, shape shoulders by binding off from each shoulder edge 4 sts 3 (2, 1) times, 5 sts 0 (1, 2) times.

FRONT
Work as for back until armhole measures 6 (6¼, 6½)"/15 (16, 16.5)cm.

Neck shaping
Next row (RS) Work 18 (19, 20) sts, join 2nd ball of yarn and bind off center 22 sts, work to end. Cont to work both sides at once, bind off 2 sts from each neck edge once, 1 st every other row 4 times. When same length as back, shape shoulders as for back.

FINISHING
Block pieces to measurements. Sew one shoulder seam. With size 5 (3.75mm) needles, pick up and k 96 (100, 102) sts evenly around one armhole edge. Work in k2, p2 rib for 1½"/4cm. Bind off in rib. Pick up and k 100 sts evenly around neck and work rib in same way. Sew other shoulder and neckband seam. Work other armhole band in same way. Sew side seams.

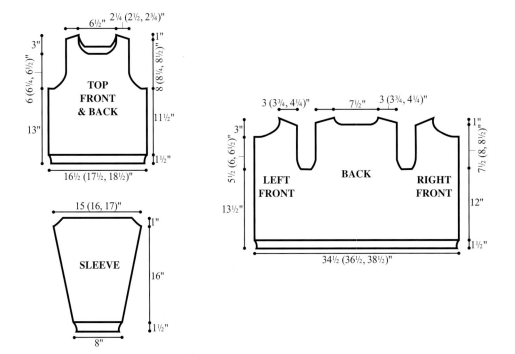

Racer-Back Tank Top

Soak up the sun in Loren Cherensky's racer-back tank. Tropical-colored yarn and easy stockinette stitching shape up this high-voltage charmer, perfect for fun-filled summer days. Shown in size Medium. The Racer-Back Tank Top first appeared in the Spring/Summer '00 issue of *Vogue Knitting*.

Racer-Back Tank Top

SIZES
To fit Small (Medium, Large). Directions are for smallest size with larger sizes in parentheses. If there is only one figure, it applies to all sizes.

KNITTED MEASUREMENTS
● Bust 33 (35, 37)"/84 (89, 94)cm
● Length 18½ (19¼, 20)"/47 (49, 51)cm

MATERIALS
● 6 (6, 7) 1¾oz/50g balls (each approx 99yd/90m) of Trendsetter Yarns *Dolcino* (acrylic myolis/polyamide 5) in #15 orange
● One pair size 10 (6mm) needles OR SIZE TO OBTAIN GAUGE

GAUGE
17 sts and 25 rows = 4"/10cm over St st using size 10 (6mm) needles.
FOR PERFECT FIT, TAKE TIME TO CHECK GAUGE.

FRONT
Cast on 64 (68, 72) sts. Work in St st, inc 1 st each side every 16th row 3 times— 70 (74, 78) sts. Work even until piece measures 11"/28cm from beg.

Armhole shaping
Bind off 5 sts at beg of next 2 rows. **Next (dec) row (RS)** K1, [p1, k1] 3 times, p2tog, k to last 9 sts, p2tog, k1, [p1, k1] 3 times. **Next row** Rib 8 sts, p to last 8 sts. rib 8 sts. Rep dec row every other row 2 (4, 6) times then every 4th row 10 times, AT SAME TIME, when armhole measures 3¾ (4½, 5¼)"/9.5 (11.5, 13.5)cm, bind off center 18 sts for neck. When 8 sts rem each side for straps after all decs, work 1 row even. Bind off.

BACK
Work as for front to armhole.

Armhole shaping
Bind off 9 sts at beg of next 2 rows—52 (56, 60) sts. **Next (dec) row (RS)** K1 [p1, k1] 3 times, p2tog, k to last 9 sts, p2tog, k1, [p1, k1] 3 times. **Next row (WS)** Rib 7 sts, k2tog, p to last 9 sts, k2tog, rib 7 sts. Rep these 2 rows until 17 sts rem (omit dec on one side on last dec). **Next row** Work 3 center sts tog. Rep this row every row until 9 sts rem. Work even on 9 sts for 1½"/4cm. Cast on 17 sts at beg of next 2 rows—43 sts. Work in k1, p1 rib for 10 rows, AT SAME TIME dec 1 st each side every other row 5 times—33 sts. Bind off loosely in rib.

FINISHING
Block pieces to measurements. Sew side seams. Sew front straps to shaped side edges of back.

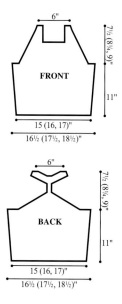

Go totally textural with Teva Durham's stylish tunic. Featuring all-over seed stitch pattern and classic shaping, this wear-everywhere essential spans the seasons and flatters every body. Shown in size Medium. The Sleeveless Seed-Stitched Top first appeared in the Spring/Summer '00 issue of *Vogue Knitting*.

Sleeveless Seed-Stitched Top

VERY EASY VERY VOGUE

SIZES
To fit Small (Medium, Large). Directions are for smallest size with larger sizes in parentheses. If there is only one figure, it applies to all sizes.

KNITTED MEASUREMENTS
● Bust 34½ (36, 39)"/87.5 (96.5, 99)cm
● Length 21¾ (22, 22½)"/55 (56, 57)cm

MATERIALS
● 7 (7, 8) 1¾oz/50g skeins (each approx 55yd/50m) of Berroco, Inc. *Pronto* (cotton/acrylic) in #4437 yellow
● Size 13 (9mm) circular needle, 24"/60cm long
● Size 10½ (6.5mm) circular needle, 16"/40cm long
● Stitch holders and markers

GAUGE
10 sts and 16 rnds = 4"/10cm over seed st pat using larger needle.
FOR PERFECT FIT, TAKE TIME TO CHECK GAUGE.

Note
When combining the options to make a different version, be sure to adjust yarn amounts accordingly.

SEED STITCH PATTERN
(over an even number of sts)
Rnd 1 *K1, p1; rep from * around. **Rnd 2** *P1, k1; rep from * around. Rep rnds 1 and 2 for seed st.
Note Sweaters are worked in rnds to the armhole, then back and forth in rows to the shoulders.

BODY
With larger circular needle, cast on 86 (90, 98) sts. Join and work in rnds of seed st for 3 rnds. **Next (dec) rnd** *Sl 1, p2tog, psso, work seed st over 40 (42, 46) sts, pm; rep from * around—82 (86, 94) sts. Work 3 rnds even. **Next (dec) rnd** *Sl 1, p2tog, psso, work seed st to marker; rep from * once. Rep last 4 rnds 4 times more—62 (66, 74) sts. Work 9 rnds even. **Next (inc) rnd** Work 2 sts in first st (inc), work seed st to 1 st before marker, work 2 sts in each of next 2 sts, work seed st to end, working 2 sts in last st—66 (70, 78) sts. Work 3 rnds even. Rep last 4 rnds 5 times more—86 (90, 98) sts. Work even until piece measures 15"/38cm from beg.

Armhole shaping
Next row (RS) K2tog tbl, work to 3 sts before marker, k1, k2tog, turn. Working back and forth on these 41 (43, 47) sts for back only, cont as foll: **Next row (WS)** K2, p2tog, work to last 4 sts, p2tog, k2. Cont with k2 selvage sts each side, dec 1 st each side every other row 3 times more—33 (35, 39) sts. Work even until armhole measures 6¾ (7, 7½)"/17 (18, 19)cm. Place sts on a holder.

FRONT
Rejoin yarn to sts for front and work as for back until armhole measures 4¾ (5, 5½)"/12 (12.5, 14)cm.

Neck shaping
Next row (RS) Work 9 (10, 12) sts, place center 15 sts on a holder for neck, join 2nd ball of yarn and work to end. Working both sides at once, dec 1 st each side of neck every other row 4 times—5 (6, 8) sts each side. Leave sts on a holder.

FINISHING
Block lightly to measurements. Weave tog 5 (6, 8) shoulder sts from holders each side using Kitchener st or knit them tog. Sew side seams.

Neckband
With larger circular needle, pick up and k 50 sts evenly around neck edge, including sts from holders. Join and work in rnds of seed st for 5 rnds. Change to smaller circular needle and work 7 more rnds of seed st. Bind off loosely.

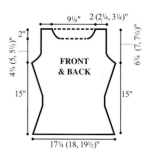

Alison Collis stitches it up with lacy openwork in fine-gauge cotton yarn. The breezy netting knits up fast, while drawstring wrists and rolled neck add to the feminine feel. Shown in size Medium. The Rolled-Neck Pullover first appeared in the Spring/Summer '96 issue of *Vogue Knitting*.

Rolled-Neck Pullover

VERY EASY VERY VOGUE

SIZES
To fit Small (Medium, Large). Directions are for smallest size with larger sizes in parentheses. If there is only one figure, it applies to all sizes.

KNITTED MEASUREMENTS
● Bust 38 (42, 46)"/96.5 (106.5, 117)cm
● Length 25 (25, 27)"/63.5 (63.5, 68.5)cm
● Sleeve width at upper arm 18 (18, 20)"/45.5 (45.5, 50.5)cm

MATERIALS
● 5 (6, 7) 1¾oz/50g balls (each approx 220yd/200m) of Skacel *Cable 5* (cotton 1) in #636 celery
● One pair each sizes 3 and 8 (3.25 and 5mm) needles OR SIZE TO OBTAIN GAUGE

GAUGE
23 sts and 22 rows to 4"/l0cm over Lace pat, using larger needles.
FOR PERFECT FIT, TAKE TIME TO CHECK GAUGE.

Lace Pat
(multiple of 6 sts, plus 1)
Row 1 K2, *yo, p3tog, yo, k3; rep from *, end yo, p3tog, yo, k2. Rep this row for Lace pat.

BACK
With larger needles, cast on 109 (121, 133) sts. Work in Lace pat for 16 (16, 17)"/40.5 (40.5, 43)cm, end with a WS row.

Armhole shaping
Bind off 7 sts at beg of next 2 rows - 95 (107, 119) sts. Work even until armhole measures 7 (7, 8)"/18 (18, 20.5)cm, end with a WS row.

Neck shaping
Next row (RS) Work 34 (38, 44) sts, join 2nd ball and bind off center 27 (31, 31) sts, work to end. Working both sides at once, bind off from each neck edge 2 sts twice. Work even until armhole measures 9 (9, 10)"/23 (23, 25.5) cm. Bind off rem 30 (34, 40) sts each side for shoulders.

FRONT
Work as for back.

SLEEVES
With larger needles, cast on 91 sts. Work in Lace pat, inc 1 st each side (working inc sts into pat) every 16th (16th, 8th) row 5 (5, 11) times, every 18th (18th, 10th) row once—103 (103, 115) sts. Work even until piece measures 19"/48cm from beg. Bind off loosely.

FINISHING
Sew right shoulder seam.

Neckband
With RS facing and smaller needles, beg at left front shoulder, *pick up and k 12 sts down side of neck, 54 (62, 62) sts along center neck (picking up 2 sts in every bound-off st), 12 sts up side of neck; rep from * for back neck - 156 (172, 172) sts. Work in St st for 2"/5cm.

Bind off. Let collar roll naturally to outside. Sew rem shoulder seam, including neckband. Set in sleeves. Sew side and sleeve seams. Pin garment to size and wet steam.

Wrist ties
(make 2)
Cut 4 strands of yam approx 7ft/213cm long. Twist strands tog, twisting ends in opposite directions, until they fold in half. Tie a knot at both ends. Thread one twisted cord through sts at each sleeve cuff, approx 1"/2.5cm above cast-on edge.

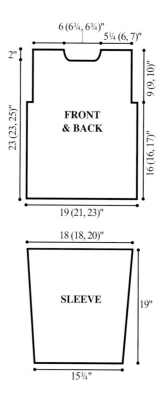

Rediscover relaxed elegance with Melissa Leapman's classic crewneck pullover. Featuring a drop-stitch cable pattern and ribbed edging, this warm-weather favorite takes textural interest to new heights. Shown in size Small. The Cropped Top first appeared in the Spring/Summer '95 issue of *Vogue Knitting*.

Cropped Top

VERY EASY VERY VOGUE

SIZES
To fit X-Small (Small, Medium, Large, X-Large). Perfect Plus sizes: [Plus 1, Plus 2, Plus 3]. Directions are for smallest size with larger sizes in parentheses. If there is only one figure, it applies to all sizes.

KNITTED MEASUREMENTS
● Bust 38 (40, 42, 44, 46)"/96.5 (101.5, 106.5, 112, 117)cm; [51, 53, 57"/ 129.5, 134.5, 144.5cm).
● Length 16 (17, 17, 18, 19)"/41 (43.5, 43.5, 46, 48.5)cm; [23, 24, 25"/58.5, 61, 63.5cm].
● Sleeve width at upper arm 15 (16, 16, 17, 18)"/38 (41, 41, 43.5, 46)cm; [20, 21, 22"/51, 53.5, 56cm].

MATERIALS
Original Yarn
● 8 (9, 9,10,10) [12, 13,15] 1¾oz/50g balls (each approx 103yd/95m) of Tahki *Linguine* (cotton 5) in #718 pale yellow
Substitute Yarn
● 7(8,8,9,9) [11,12,13] 1¾oz/50g (each approx 121yd/111m) of Skacel *Sirenetta* (cotton/acrylic) in #2
● Size 9 (5.5mm) needles OR SIZE TO OBTAIN GAUGE
● Cable needle

Note
The original yarn used for this sweater is no longer available. A comparable substitute has been made, which is available at the time of printing. Check gauge of substitute yarns very carefully before beginning.

GAUGE
34 sts and 35 rows = 4"/10cm over chart pat (slightly stretched) using larger needles. FOR PERFECT FIT, TAKE TIME TO CHECK GAUGE.

STITCH GLOSSARY
23 sts and 26 rows to 4"/10cm over cable pat using size 9 (5½mm) needles.

STITCH GLOSSARY
Rib pat (multiple of 6 sts plus 2 extra)
Row 1 (RS) K1, *k3, p3; rep from *, end k1. Rep row 1 for rib pat.
Dropped stitch cable
(multiple of 6 sts plus 2 extra) **Rows 1 and 3 (RS)** Knit. **Rows 2 and 4** Purl. **Row 5** K1, *k next st wrapping yarn twice around needle; rep from *, end k1. **Row 6** K1, sl 3 to cable needle (cn) letting extra loops drop, hold to front of work, p3 letting extra loops drop; p3 from cn; rep from *, end k1. Rep rows 1-6 for dropped stitch cable pat.
Note
Two selvage sts are included and are not reflected in finished measurements. Note for Perfect Plus sizes only: Unless otherwise specified, foll all instructions as given for regular sizes. Numbers for Perfect Plus sizes are in brackets. If there is only one number or one set of instructions, it applies to all Perfect Plus sizes.

BACK
Cast on 110 (116, 122, 128, 134) [146, 152, 164] sts. Work 4 rows in rib pat. Work in dropped stitch cable pat until piece measures 7½ (8, 8, 8½, 9)"/19 (20.5, 20.5, 21.5, 23)cm [12, 12½,13"/ 30.5, 32, 33cm] from beg, end with a WS row.

Armhole shaping
Bind off 6 [12] sts at beg of next 2 rows, and for Perfect Plus sizes only: dec 1 st each side every row [9, 6, 6] times—98 (104, 110, 116,122) [104,116,128] sts. Work even until armhole measures 7½ (8, 8, 8½, 9)"/19 (20.5, 20.5, 21.5, 23)cm [10, 10½, 11"/25.5, 27, 28cm], end with a WS row.

Shoulder shaping
Bind off 9 (10, 11, 12, 13) [9, 11, 12] sts at beg of next 4 rows, 11 (11, 12, 12, 13) [10, 10,13] sts at beg of next 2 rows. Bind off rem 40 (42, 42, 44, 44) [48, 52, 54] sts.

FRONT
Work as for back. When armhole measures 6½ (7, 7, 7½, 8)"/16.5 (18,18,19, 20.5)cm [8, 8½, 9"/20.5, 21.5, 23cm], end with a WS row.

Neck shaping
Next row (RS) Work 41 (43, 46, 48, 51) [42, 46, 51] sts, join 2nd ball of yarn and bind off 16 (18, 18, 20, 20) [20, 24, 26] sts, work to end. Working both sides at once, bind off from each neck edge 6 [6] sts once, 3 [3] sts once, then dec 1 [1] st at each neck edge every row 3 [5] times. When piece measures same as back to shoulders, shape shoulder as for back.

SLEEVES
Cast on 74 (74, 80, 80, 80) [104, 116, 116] sts. Work 4 rows in rib pat. Work pats and incs simultaneously as foll: For regular sizes only: Work in dropped stitch cable pat, AT SAME TIME, inc 1 st each side (working inc sts into cable

pat) every 4th row 3 (9, 0, 7,12) times, every 6th row 4 (1, 7, 3, 1)—88 (94, 94, 100, 106). For Perfect Plus sizes only: Work in dropped stitch cable pat, AT SAME TIME, inc 1 st each side (working inc sts into cable pat) every 8th row [6, 0, 0] times, every10th row [0, 2, 5] times—[116,120,126] sts. For all sizes: Work even until sleeve measures 7½ (8, 8, 8½, 8½)"/19 (20.5, 20.5, 21.5, 21.5)cm [8½, 9, 10"/21.5, 23, 25.5cm] from beg. Bind off all sts.

FINISHING
Block pieces lightly. Sew left shoulder seam.

Neckband
With RS facing, pick up and k41 (43, 43, 45, 45) [49, 53, 56] sts along back neck, 45 (49, 49, 53, 53) [55, 57, 60] sts along front neck—86 (92, 92, 98, 98) [104, 110, 116] sts. Work 6 rows in rib pat. Bind off in rib pat. Sew left shoulder

seam and neckband. Sew top of sleeves to armhole. Sew bound off sts of body to side edges of sleeves. Sew side and sleeve seams.

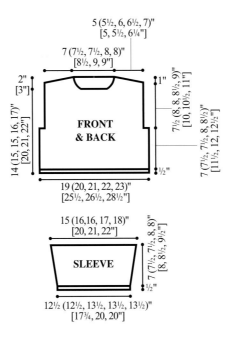

5 (5½, 6, 6½, 7)"
[5, 5½, 6¼"]

7 (7½, 7½, 8, 8)"
[8½, 9, 9"]

2"
[3"]

1"

7½ (8, 8, 8½, 9)"
[10, 10½, 11"]

FRONT & BACK

14 (15, 15, 16, 17)"
[20, 21, 22"]

7 (7½, 7½, 8, 8½)"
[11½, 12, 12½"]

½"

19 (20, 21, 22, 23)"
[25½, 26½, 28½"]

15 (16,16, 17, 18)"
[20, 21, 22"]

SLEEVE

7 (7½, 7½, 8, 8)"
[8, 8½, 9½"]

½"

12½ (12½, 13½, 13½, 13½)"
[17¾, 20, 20"]

Sleeveless Pullover

Simply chic. Paired with linen pants or a long skirt, Rosemary Drysdale's ultra-easy stockinette top goes from casual to elegant with ease. Feeling daring? Go for the slit-front and cropped length option. Both shown in size Medium. The Sleeveless Pullover first appeared in the Spring/Summer '00 issue of *Vogue Knitting*.

Sleeveless Pullover

VERY EASY VERY VOGUE

SIZES
To fit Small (Medium, Large, X-Large, XX-Large). Directions are for smallest size with larger sizes in parentheses. If there is only one figure, it applies to all sizes.

KNITTED MEASUREMENTS
Shorter version
● Lower edge 37 (40, 44, 49, 53)"/94 (101.5, 111.5, 124.5, 134.5)cm
● Bust 35 (38, 42, 46, 50)"/89 (96.5, 106.5, 117, 127)cm
● Length 16½ (17, 17½, 17½, 18)"/41.5 (43, 44.5, 44.5, 45.5)cm
Longer version
● Lower edge 39 (42, 46, 51, 55)"/99 (106.5, 117, 129.5, 139.5)cm
● Bust 35 (38, 42, 46, 50)"/89 (96.5, 106.5, 117, 127)cm
● Length 23½ (24, 24½, 24½, 25)"59.5 (61, 62.5, 62.5, 63.5)cm

MATERIALS
Longer version
● 11 (11, 13, 14, 15) balls 1¾oz/50g (each approx 120yd/110m) of Filatura Di Crosa/Stacy Charles Collection *Brilla* (viscose/cotton 2) in #324 ecru
Shorter version
● 7 (8, 9, 10, 10) balls in #324 ecru
Both versions
● One pair size 10 (6mm) needles OR SIZE TO OBTAIN GAUGE
● Size 10 (6mm) circular needle, 16"/40cm long
● Stitch holders

GAUGE
16 sts and 20 rows = 4"/10cm over St st using size 10 (6mm) needles and 2 strands held tog.
FOR PERFECT FIT, TAKE TIME TO CHECK GAUGE.

Note
When combining the options to make a different version, be sure to adjust yarn amounts accordingly.

BACK
With 2 strands held tog, cast on 78 (84, 92, 102, 110) sts. Work in St st for 4"/10cm, end with a WS row. **Next (dec) row (RS)** K1, k2tog tbl, k to last 3 sts, k2tog, k1. [Work 15 rows even. Rep dec row] 3 (3, 3, 4, 4) times—70 (76, 84, 92, 100) sts. Work even until piece measures 16½"/42cm from beg, end with a WS row.

Armhole shaping
Bind off 3 (4, 5, 6, 6) sts at beg of next 2 rows, 2 sts at beg of next 0 (0, 0, 4, 6) rows. **Next row** K2, SKP, work to last 4 sts, k2tog, k2. Work 1 row even. Rep last 2 rows 3 (4, 5, 3, 3) times more—56 (58, 62, 64, 68) sts. Work even until armhole measures 7 (7½, 8, 8, 8½)"/17 (19, 20.5, 20.5, 21.5)cm end with a WS row.

Neck and shoulder shaping
Bind off 11 (12, 14, 15, 17) sts at beg of next 2 rows. Place center 34 sts on holder for neck.

FRONT
Work as for back.

FINISHING
Block pieces to measurements. Sew shoulder seams

Neckband
With RS facing and circular needle, pick up and k 68 sts around neck. Work in rnds of St st until neck measures 4"/10cm. Bind off loosely. Sew side seams. Fold band in half to WS and sl st bound-off edge to inside neck edge.

SHORTER VERSION

BACK
With 2 strands held tog, cast on 74 (80, 88, 98, 106) sts. Work as for longer version, working side decs as foll: Work 16 (16, 16, 10, 10) rows even. Work dec row on next WS row. [Work 15 (15, 15, 19, 19) rows even. Work dec row 1 (1, 1, 2, 2) times—70 (76, 84, 92, 100) sts. Complete as for back.

Left front
With 2 strands held tog, cast on 37 (40, 44, 49, 53) sts. Work in St st always k first st of p row. Work side shaping as for back. When piece measures 7½"/19cm form beg, place sts on holder.

Right front
Work as for left front, reversing shaping and k the first p st at center front (last st of p row). Work across 35 (38, 42, 46, 50) sts of left front, work across 35 (38, 42, 46, 50) sts of right front—70 (76, 84, 92, 100) sts. Complete as for back.

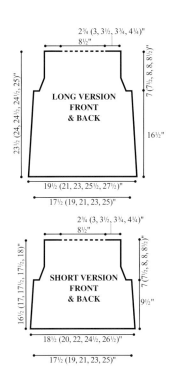

2¾ (3, 3½, 3¾, 4¼)"

8½"

23½ (24, 24½, 24½, 25)"

7 (7½, 8, 8, 8½)"

**LONG VERSION
FRONT
& BACK**

16½"

19½ (21, 23, 25½, 27½)"

17½ (19, 21, 23, 25)"

2¾ (3, 3½, 3¾, 4¼)"

8½"

16½ (17, 17½, 17½, 18)"

7 (7½, 8, 8, 8½)"

**SHORT VERSION
FRONT
& BACK**

9½"

18½ (20, 22, 24½, 26½)"

17½ (19, 21, 23, 25)"

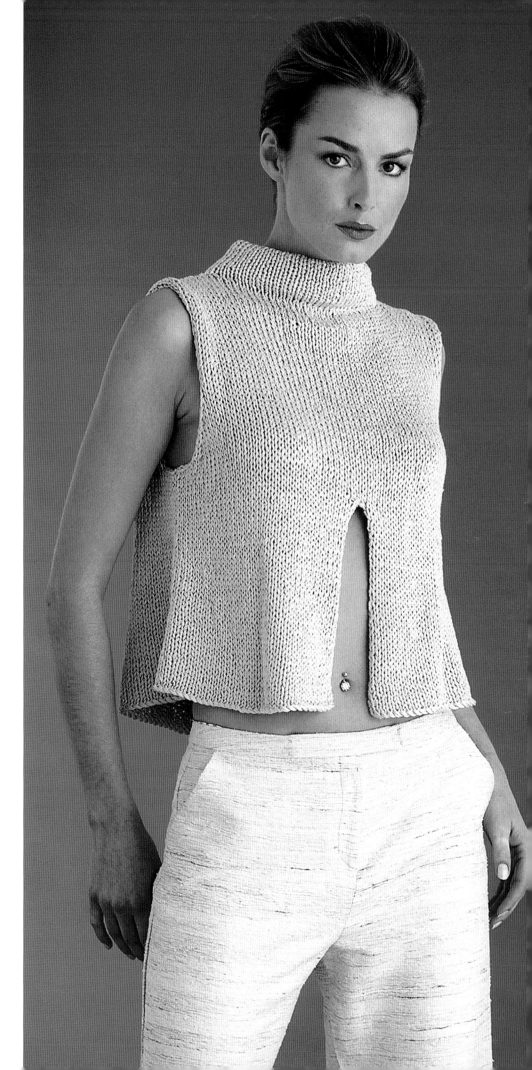

Smart and sophisticated, Viola Carol's classic twin set is an enduring fashion favorite. Stitched in a season-spanning cotton/wool blend and easy stockinette, it's sure to become a wardrobe staple. Shown in size Medium. The Summer Twin Set first appeared in the Spring/Summer '99 issue of *Vogue Knitting*.

Summer Twin Set

VERY EASY VERY VOGUE

SIZES
To fit Small (Medium, Large, X-Large). Directions are for smallest size with larger sizes in parentheses. If there is only one figure, it applies to all sizes.

KNITTED MEASUREMENTS
Top
● Bust 33 (35½, 38, 40)"/83.5 (90, 96.5, 101.5)cm
● Length 17¼ (18, 18½, 18¾)"/45 (45.5, 47, 47.5)cm
Cardigan
● Bust (buttoned) 34 (36½, 39, 41)"/86 (92.5, 99, 104)cm
● Length 19¼ (19½, 20, 20¼)"/48.5 (49.5, 50.5,51)cm
● Upper arm 12½ (13,13¼, 14¼)"/32 (33, 35, 36)cm

MATERIALS
● 10 (10, 11, 12) 3½oz/100g skeins (each approx 215yd/197m) of Brown Sheep *Cotton Fleece* (cotton/wool 4) in #CW-640 pale green
● One pair each sizes 8 and 10 (5 and 6mm) needles OR SIZE TO OBTAIN GAUGE
● Four ⅞"/22mm buttons

GAUGE
14 sts and 19 rows = 4"/10cm over twisted knit st using double strand of yarn held tog and larger needles.
FOR PERFECT FIT, TAKE TIME TO CHECK GAUGE.

Note
Use a double strand of yarn held tog throughout.

TWISTED KNIT STITCH
Row 1 K1 (selvage st), *k1 tbl; rep from * to last st, k1 (selvage st).
Row 2 K1, p to last st, k1. Rep these 2 rows for twisted knit st.

TOP

BACK
With smaller needles and double strand of yarn held tog, cast on 58 (62, 66, 70) sts. **Row 1 (RS)** *K1 tbl, p1; rep from * to end. Rep this row for k1, p1 twisted rib for 2 more rows. Change to larger needles. **Next row (WS)** K1, p to last st, k1. Cont in twisted knit st until piece measures 5"/12.5cm from beg. **Next row (RS)** K1, M 1, work twisted st to last st, M1, k1—60 (64, 68, 72) sts. Work even until piece measures 10½"/26.5cm from beg.

Armhole shaping
Bind off 5 (5, 6, 6) sts at beg of next 2 rows, dec 1 st each side every other row (inside selvage sts) 3 (4, 4, 5) times—44 (46,48,50) sts. Work even until armhole measures 6½ (6¾, 7¼, 7½)"/16.5 (17, 18.5, 19)cm.

Neck shaping
Next row (RS) K12 (13 14, 14) sts, join another double strand of yarn and bind off center 20 (20, 20, 22) sts, work to end. Working both sides at once, bind off 3 sts from each neck edge once, AT SAME TIME, when armhole measures 7 (7½, 8, 8¼)"/18.5 (19, 20.5, 21)cm, bind off 9 (10, 11, 11) sts each side for shoulders.

FRONT
Work as for back until armhole measures 4¾ (5, 5½, 5¾)"/12 (12.5, 14, 14.5)cm

Neck shaping
Next row (RS) K17 (18, 19, 19) sts, join another double strand of yarn and bind off center 10 (10, 10, 12) sts, work to end. Working both sides at once, bind off 2 sts from each neck edge every other row 3 times, dec 1 st every other row twice. When same length as back, bind off rem 9 (10, 11, 11) sts each side for shoulders.

FINISHING
Block pieces to measurements. Sew left shoulder seam. With smaller needles and double strand of yarn held tog, pick up and k 73 (73, 73, 77) sts evenly around neck edge. Work in k1, p1 twisted rib for 3 rows. Bind off in rib. Sew other shoulder and neckband seam. Sew side seams.

Pocket
With larger needles and double strand of yarn held tog, cast on 12 sts. Work in twisted knit st (omitting selvage sts) for 3"/7.5cm. Bind off 3 sts at beg of next 2 rows. Bind off rem 6 sts. Sew pocket to lower left front as in photo.

CARDIGAN

BACK

With smaller needles and double strand of yarn held tog, cast on 58 (62, 66, 70) sts. **Row 1 (RS)** *K1 tbl, p1; rep from * to end. Rep this row for k1, p1 twisted rib for 8 more rows. Change to larger needles. **Next row (WS)** K1, p to last st, k1. Cont in twisted knit st until piece measures 4"/10cm from beg. **Next row (RS)** K1, M1, work twisted st to last st. Ml, k1. Rep this inc row every 4"/10cm once more—62 (66, 70, 74) sts. Work even until piece measures 11½"/29cm from beg.

Armhole shaping

Bind off 4 (5, 5, 5) sts at beg of next 2 rows. **Next row (RS)** K1, SKP, work twisted knit st to last 3 sts, k2tog, k1. Work 1 row even. Rep these 2 rows 1 (1,2, 3) times more—50 (52, 54, 56) sts. Work even until armhole measures 7 (7¼, 7¾, 8)"/17.5 (18.5, 19, 20.5)cm.

Neck shaping

Next row (RS) K14 (15, 16, 16), join another double strand of yarn and bind off center 22 (22, 22. 24) sts. Work to end. Working both sides at once. bind off 3 sts from each neck edge once, AT SAME TIME, when armhole measures 7¼ (8, 8½, 8¾)"/19.5 (20.5, 21.5, 22)cm, bind off 11(12, 13, 13) sts each side for shoulders.

LEFT FRONT

With smaller needles and double strand of yarn held tog, cast on 32 (34, 36, 38) sts. **Row 1 (RS)** *K1 tbl, p1; rep from *, end last rep k1 (selvage st). Cont in twisted rib st for 8 more rows. Change to larger needles. Cont in twisted knit st as on back (having a k1 selvage st at beg and end of every row) and inc 1 st at beg of RS rows every 4"/10cm twice—34 (36, 38, 40) sts. Work even until piece measures 11½"/29cm from beg.

Armhole shaping

Bind off 4 (5,5,5) sts from armhole edge once, then dec 1 st (as on back) every other row 2 (2, 3, 4) times—28 (29, 30, 31) sts. Work even until armhole measures 5¼ (5½, 6, 6¼)"/13.5 (14, 15, 16)cm.

Neck shaping

Next row (WS) Bind off 12 sts, work to end. Cont to dec 1 st from neck edge every row twice, every other row 3 (3, 3, 4) times. When same length as back, bind off rem 11 (12, 13, 13) sts for shoulder. Place marker for 4 buttons at 4 sts in from center front, the first one at ½"/1.25cm above lower rib, the last one at ½"/1.25cm from neck shaping and the other 2 evenly spaced between.

RIGHT FRONT

Work to correspond to left front only working buttonholes opposite markers as foll: **Buttonhole row (RS)** Working in pat, k3, k2tog, yo, work to end.

SLEEVES

With smaller needles and double strand of yarn held tog, cast on 36 (38, 40, 42) sts. Work in k1, p1 twisted rib for 8 rows. Change to larger needles and cont in twisted knit st inc 1 st each side every 1 Oth row (inside selvage sts) 5 times—46 (48, 50, 52) sts. Work even until piece measures 17"/43cm from beg.

Cap shaping

Bind off 5 sts at beg of next 2 rows. Dec 1 st each side of every other row 8 (9, 10, 11) times. Bind off 3 sts at beg of next 4 rows. Bind off rem 8 sts.

FINISHING

Block pieces to measurements. Sew shoulder seams. With smaller needles and double strand of yarn held tog, pick up and k 73 (73, 73, 77) sts evenly around neck edge. Work in twisted rib for 3 rows. Bind off in rib. Sew sleeves into armholes. Sew side and sleeve seams. Sew on buttons.

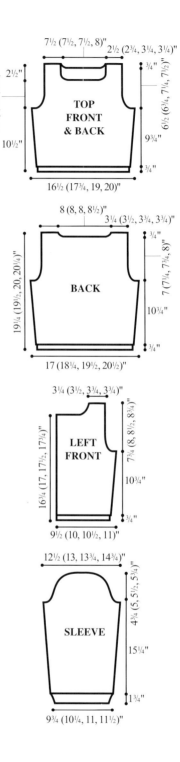

Warm and Comfy

Soft, sculptural and totally textural. Revel in comfort with these contemporary classics—cool designs that go beyond the basics.

Easy does it. Norah Gaugan's smart and casual pullover is knit circularly to the underarm and topped with a striking Möbius collar. Shown in size Medium. Worked in a beautiful brushed mohair blend, the Sweater with Möbius Collar first appeared in the Winter '01/'02 issue of *Vogue Knitting*.

Sweater with Möbius Collar

VERY EASY VERY VOGUE

SIZES
Sized for X-Small, Small, Medium, Large, X-Large and shown in size Medium. Directions are for smallest size with larger sizes in parentheses. If there is only one figure, it applies to all sizes.

KNITTED MEASUREMENTS
● Bust 35½ (38, 40½, 45, 48½)"/90 (96.5, 102.5, 114, 123)cm
● Length 22 (22½, 23, 25, 25½)"/56 (57, 58.5, 63.5, 64.5)cm
● Upper arm 12 (12½, 13, 13½, 14)"/30.5 (31.5, 33, 34, 35.5)cm

MATERIALS
● 11 (12, 13, 15, 16) 1¾oz/50g balls (each approx 120yd/110m) of Adrienne Vittadini/JCA *Sara* (wool/mohair/nylon 4) in #1531 purple
● Size 10½ (6.5mm) circular needles, 24" and 16"/60 and 40cm long OR SIZE TO OBTAIN GAUGE
● Size 7 (4.5mm) circular needle, 16"/40cm long
● Stitch holders and markers

GAUGE
13 sts and 17 rows = 4"/10cm over St st using size 10½ (6.5mm) needles.
FOR PERFECT FIT, TAKE TIME TO CHECK GAUGE.

Note
1 When working in rnds, knit every rnd.
2 Use 2 strands of yarn held together for body, sleeves and yoke. Use 1 strand for collar.

BODY
With longer size 10½ (6.5mm) needle and 2 strands of yarn held tog, cast on 140 (148, 156, 170, 182) sts. Join, taking care not to twist sts on needle. Place markers for beg and center of rnd, and slip markers every rnd. Work in St st for 3"/7.5cm. **Next (dec) rnd** K2, k2tog, work to within 4 sts of center marker, SSK, k4, k2tog, work to last 4 sts of rnd, SSK, k2. Rep dec rnd every 8th rnd 5 times more—116 (124, 132, 146, 158) sts. Work even until piece measures 15 (15, 15, 16, 16)"/38 (38, 38, 40.5, 40.5)cm from beg. **Next 2 rnds** Work to last 3 (4, 5, 4, 4) sts of rnd, bind off 6 (8, 10, 8, 8) sts, work to 3 (4, 5, 4, 4) sts of center marker, bind off 6 (8, 10, 8, 8) sts,

work to end of rnd. Place rem sts on a holder.

SLEEVES
With shorter size 10½ (6.5mm) needle and 2 strands of yarn held tog, cast on 38 (40, 42, 44, 46) sts. Join, taking care not to twist sts on needle. Place marker for beg of rnd and slip marker every rnd. Work in St st for 18"/45.5cm. **Next 2 rnds** Work to last 4 sts of rnd, bind off 8 sts, work to end of rnd, place rem sts on a holder.

YOKE
K across 30 (32, 34, 36, 38) sts of first sleeve, pm, 52 (54, 56, 65, 71) sts of front, pm, 30 (32, 34, 36, 38) sts of 2nd sleeve, pm, 52 (54, 56, 65, 71) sts of back—164 (172, 180, 202, 218) sts. Pm for beg of rnd. K 3 rnds. **Next (dec) rnd** K2, k2tog, [work to 4 sts before next marker, SSK, k4, k2tog] 3 times, work to last 4 sts of rnd, SSK, k2. Rep dec rnd every other rnd 9 (10, 11, 13, 15) times more—84 (84, 84, 90, 90) sts. Bind off.

COLLAR
With smaller circular needle and 1 strand of yarn, cast on 64 sts. Join,

taking care not to twist sts on needle.
K until piece measures 28 (28, 28, 29½,
29½)"/71 (71, 71, 75, 75)cm.
Lay piece flat horizontally and fold cast
on edge over 180 degrees (to make
double thickness) and graft. Then fold,
making a "v" in the middle. Graft cast-on
edge to last row.

FINISHING

Block piece to measurements. Sew collar to neck, placing seam in center back
and centering the fold in front (see
photo). Sew underarms.

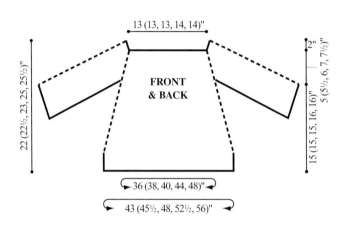

Textured Ribbed Pullover

Cross over to comfort in Jennifer Vafakos's relaxed turtleneck. Columns of chunky ribs intersect across the chest, it all knits up quick in chunky yarn. Shown in size Medium. The Textured Ribbed Pullover first appeared in the Winter '98/'99 issue of *Vogue Knitting*.

Textured Ribbed Pullover

VERY EASY VERY VOGUE

SIZES
To fit Small (Medium, Large, X-Large). Directions are for smallest size with larger sizes in parentheses. If there is only one figure, it applies to all sizes.

KNITTED MEASUREMENTS
● Bust 40 (43, 46, 50)"/101.5 (109, 117, 127)cm
● Length 26 (26½, 27, 27½)"/66 (67, 68.5, 69.5))cm
● Upper arm 16 (17, 18, 19)"/41 (43, 46, 48)cm

MATERIALS
● 15 (16, 17, 18) 3½oz/100g balls (each approx 54yd/50m) of Colinette *Apollo* (cotton/viscose/wool/silk 5) in mushroom
● One pair each sizes 10 and 11 (6 and 8mm) needles OR SIZE TO OBTAIN GAUGE
● Size 10 (6mm) circular needle 16"/40cm long
● Two cable needles (cn)
● Stitch holders

GAUGE
10 sts and 16 rows = 4"/10cm over k2, p2 rib, slightly stretched, using larger needles FOR PERFECT FIT, TAKE TIME TO CHECK GAUGE.

STITCH GLOSSARY
K2, P2 Rib
(multiple of 4 sts)
Row 1 (RS) *K1, p2, k1; rep from * to end.
Row 2 K the knit sts and p the purl sts.

Rep row 2 for k2, p2 rib.
C6 Sl 2 sts to cn and hold to front of work, sl next 2 sts to a 2nd cn and hold to back of work, k2 sts from LH needle, p2 from back cn, k2 from front cn.

BACK
With larger needles, cast on 56 (60, 64, 68) sts. Change to smaller needles and work in k2, p2 rib for 2"/5cm as foll: For sizes Small and Large P1, *k2, p2; rep from *, end k2, p1. For sizes Medium and X-Large *K1, p2, k1; rep from * to end. Change to larger needles and cont in rib, dec 1 st each side every 18th row 3 times—50 (54, 58, 62) sts. Work even until piece measures 17"/43cm from beg.

Armhole shaping
Bind off 5 (5, 6, 6) sts at beg of next 2 rows—40 (44, 46, 50) sts. Work even until armhole measures 8 (8½, 9, 9½)"/20.5 (21.5, 23, 24)cm.

Shoulder shaping
Bind off 5 (6, 7, 7) sts at beg of next 2 rows, 6 (7, 7, 8) sts at beg of next 2 rows. Place rem 18 (18, 18, 20) sts on a holder for back neck.

FRONT
Work as for back until armhole measures 2"/5cm, end with a WS row.
Cable row (RS)
For size Small P1, C6, [p2, C6] 4 times, p1. For size Medium K1, [p2, C6] 5 times, p2, k1. For size Large K2, p2, [C6, p2] 5 times, k2. For size X-Large [P2, C6] 6 times, p2. Cont in rib until armhole measures 7 (7½, 8, 8½)"/18 (19, 20.5, 21.5)cm, end with a WS row.

Neck shaping
Next row (RS) Work 15 (17, 18, 19) sts, join 2nd ball of yarn and place center 10 (10, 10, 12) sts on a holder, work to end. Working both sides at once, bind off 2 sts from each neck edge twice, AT SAME TIME, when same length as back to shoulder, shape shoulders as for back.

SLEEVES
With larger needles, cast on 32 sts. Change to smaller needles and work in k2, p2 rib for 2"/5cm. Change to larger needles and cont in rib, inc 1 st each side (working inc sts into rib) every 16th (12th, 8th, 8th) row 4 (3, 5, 8) times, every 0 (14th, 12th, 0) row twice—40 (42, 46, 48) sts. Work even until piece measures 20"/50.5cm from beg. Bind off all sts.

FINISHING
Block pieces to measurements. Sew shoulder seams.

Turtleneck
With RS facing and circular needle, work 18 (18, 18, 20) sts from back neck holder, pick up and k 6 (6, 6, 8) sts along left front neck, work 10 (10, 10, 12) sts from front neck holder, pick up and k6 (6, 6, 8) sts along right front neck—40 (40, 40, 48) sts. Cont in rib for 7"/17.5cm. With larger needle, bind off loosely in rib. Sew top of sleeves to armholes, sewing last 2"/5cm at top of sleeve to bound-off armhole sts. Sew side and sleeve seams.

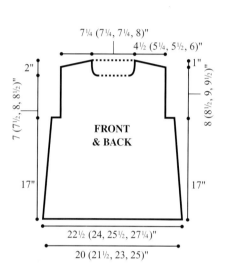

7¼ (7¼, 7¼, 8)"

4½ (5¼, 5½, 6)"

2"

1"

7 (7½, 8, 8½)"

8 (8½, 9, 9½)"

**FRONT
& BACK**

17"

17"

22½ (24, 25½, 27¼)"

20 (21½, 23, 25)"

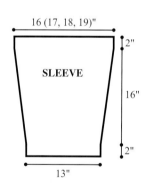

16 (17, 18, 19)"

2"

SLEEVE

16"

2"

13"

No time to fuss with fashion? Kelly Overbey's stylish ribbed boatneck pullover works up fast and fashionable in two shades of worsted yarn with a wonderful hint of bouclé. Shown in size Small. The Ribbed Pullover first appeared in the Fall '00 issue of *Vogue Knitting*.

Ribbed Pullover

VERY EASY VERY VOGUE

SIZES
To fit Small (Medium, Large). Directions are for smallest size with larger sizes in parentheses. If there is only one figure, it applies to all sizes.

KNITTED MEASUREMENTS
● Bust 33 (36, 38)"/84 (91.5, 96.5)cm
● Length 17 (17½, 18)"/43 (44.5, 45.5)cm
● Upper arm 11 (11½, 12½)"/28 (29, 32)cm

MATERIALS
● 8 (9, 9) 1¾oz/50g balls (each approx 83yd/77m) of Naturally/S.R. Kertzer Ltd. *Café* (wool/alpaca/mohair/nylon 4) in #713 tan (MC)
● 3 balls in #710 cream (CC)
● One pair each sizes 7 and 8 (4.5 and 5mm) needles OR SIZE TO OBTAIN GAUGE
● One set (5) size 7 (4.5mm) dpn

GAUGE
20 sts and 24 rows = 4"/10cm over k2, p2 rib using smaller needles.
FOR PERFECT FIT, TAKE TIME TO CHECK GAUGE.

Notes
1 Larger, size 8 (5mm) needles are used for cast-on edge only.
2 For closing up holes, if the wrapped st is a knit, insert RH needle under the wrap and the st on the needle, then ktog the wrap and st. If st is a purl, sl the st, lift the wrap from the front and place on LH needle, pass slipped st back to LH needle and p st and wrapped st tog.

BACK
With MC and larger needles, cast on 82 (90, 94) sts. P 1 row. Change to smaller needles. **Row 1 (RS)** K2, *p2, k2; rep from * to end. **Row 2** K the knit sts and p the purl sts. Cont in k2, p2 rib until piece measures 10½"/26.5cm from beg.

Armhole shaping
Bind off 5 (5, 6) sts at beg of next 2 rows. Dec 1 st each side of next row then every other row 2 (5, 5) times more—66 (68, 70) sts. Work even until armhole measures 2½ (3, 3½)"/6.5 (7.5, 9)cm. Change to CC and cont in rib for 12 more rows.

Neck shaping
Note
The neck is shaped using short rows. For short row wrapping at end of rows: If the last st worked is a knit st, bring yarn to front, sl 1 purlwise, yarn to back and return slipped st to LH needle. If the st worked is a purl st, bring yarn to back, sl 1 purlwise, yarn to front and return slipped st to LH needle.

Right shoulder
Row 1 (RS) Work 24 sts, turn, leaving rem sts unworked. **Row 2** and all even rows K the knit sts and p the purl sts. **Row 3** Work 19 sts, turn. **Row 5** Work 15 sts, turn. **Row 7** Work 12 sts, turn. **Row 9** Work 10 sts, turn. **Row 11** Work 8 sts, turn. **Row 13** Work 6 sts, turn. Work one more WS row. Cut yarn for sewing shoulder seam later and rejoin yarn to beg of WS row to work left shoulder short rows.

Left shoulder
Row 1 (WS) Work 24 sts, turn, leaving rem sts unworked. Work next 13 short rows as for right shoulder, only reversing RS and WS rows. Cut yarn at end for sewing shoulder seams and sl all 66 (68, 70) sts to a holder to be worked later.

FRONT
Work as for back.

Join front and back
Matching front and back with WS tog, graft tog 6 sts of front and back shoulders tog each side using Kitchener st. Sl rem 108 (112, 116) sts onto dpn to work in rnds. **Rnd 1** Beg at left shoulder seam, *taking 1 st from front and 1 st from back, k2tog, pm each side of this st, work in rib (working short row wraps as described in note) to next shoulder, rep from * once. **Rnd 2** Work even. Rnd 3 *Work rib to 2 sts before marker, SKP, k1, k2tog; rep from * once, rib to end. Rep this rnd 5 times more. Bind off knitwise with larger needle.

SLEEVES
With MC and larger needles, cast on 38 (38, 42) sts. P 1 row. Change to smaller needles. Work in k2, p2 rib, inc 1 st each side every 12th (10th, 10th) row 8 (10, 10) times—54 (58, 62) sts. Work even until piece measures 17"/43cm from beg.

Cap shaping

Bind off 5 sts at beg of next 2 rows. Dec 1 st each side of next row then every other row 10 (12, 14) times more. Bind off 2 sts at beg of next 4 rows. Work 2 rows even. Bind off rem 14 sts. AT SAME TIME, when cap shaping measures 2½ (3, 3½)"/6.5 (7.5, 9)cm, change to cc.

FINISHING

Block pieces to measurements. Set in sleeves. Sew side and sleeve seams.

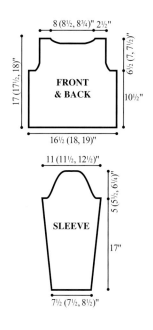

Perfect for beginners, Nicky Epstein's color-charged pullover offers a quick lesson in style. Loose ribbing, foldback cuffs and an airy turtleneck flatter all body types. Shown in size 36. The Easy Turtleneck Pullover first appeared in the Fall/Winter '86 issue of *Vogue Knitting*.

Easy Turtleneck Pullover

VERY EASY VERY VOGUE

SIZES
To fit 32 (34, 36, 38)"/81 (86, 91, 96)cm bust. Directions are for smallest size with larger sizes in parentheses. If there is only one figure, it applies to all sizes.

KNITTED MEASUREMENTS
● Bust 39 (41, 43, 45)"/98 (102, 108, 113) cm
● Length 23 (24,25,26)"/58.5 (60.5, 63.5, 65.5)cm
● Sleeve width at upper arm 17(18,18, 19)"/43 (45,45,48)cm

MATERIALS
Original Yarn
● 14 (14, 14, 15) 1¾oz/50g balls (each approx 80yd/73m) of Bernat *Musetta* (wool/mohair/acrylic 6) in color #11423 pink/purple tweed
Substitute Yarn
● 6 (6, 7) 3½oz/100g balls (each approx 190yd/180m) of Colinette Yarns/Unique Kolours *Mohair* (mohair/wool/nylon 4) in #72 tapis
● One pair each sizes 7 and 9 (4.5 and 5.5mm) needles OR SIZE TO OBTAIN GIVEN GAUGE
● Stitch markers

Note
The original yarn used for this sweater is no longer available. A comparable substitute has been made, which is available at the time of printing. Check gauge of substitute yarns very carefully before beginning.

GAUGE
16 sts and 20 rows to 4"/10cm over rib pat (slightly stretched) using size 9 (5.5mm) needles.
FOR PERFECT FIT, TAKE TIME TO CHECK GAUGE.

BACK
With smaller needles, cast on 78 (82, 86, 90)sts. **Bib row 1 (RS)** P2, *k2, p2; rep from * to end. **Rib row 2** K2, *p2, k2; rep from * to end. Rep rows 1 and 2 for rib pat for 4710cm.Change to larger needles. Cont in rib pat until piece measures 23 (24, 25, 26)758.5 (60.5, 63.5, 65.5)cm from beg.

Shoulder shaping
Bind off 19 (20, 22, 23) sts at beg of next 2 rows—40 (42, 42, 44) sts.

Turtleneck
Cont in rib pat on these sts for 10"/25.5cm. Bind off in rib.

FRONT
Work as for back.

SLEEVES
With smaller needles, cast on 38 (42, 42, 46) sts. Work rib pat as for back, for 8720.5cm, end with a WS row. Change to larger needles.
Beg inc: Row 1 (RS) Inc 1 st in first st, rib to last st, inc 1 st in last st. **Row 2** P1, *k2, p2; rep from *, end k2, p1. **Row 3** K1, *p2, k2; rep from *, end p2, k1. **Row 4** Rep row 2. **Row 5** Rep row 1. **Row 6** P2, *k2, p2; rep from * to end. **Row 7** K2, *p2, k2; rep from * to end. **Row 8** Rep row 6. **Row 9** Rep row 1. **Row 10** K1, *p2, k2; rep from *, end p2, k1. **Row 11** P1, *k2, p2; rep from *, end k2, p1. **Row 12** Rep row 10. **Row 13** Rep row 1. **Row 14** K2, *p2, k2; rep from * to end. **Row 15** P2, *k2, p2; rep from * to end. **Row 16** Rep row 14. Rep these 16 rows twice more, then rows 1-9 once more—68 (72, 72, 76) sts. Work even until piece measures 21 (21, 22, 22)"/53.5 (53.5, 56, 56)cm from beg. Bind off all sts.

FINISHING
Block pieces to measurements. Sew shoulder and turtleneck seams. Place markers 8½ (9,9, 9½)"/ 21.5 (22.5, 22.5, 24)cm down from shoulder seam on front and back for armholes. Sew top of sleeve to front and back between markers. Sew side and sleeve seams.

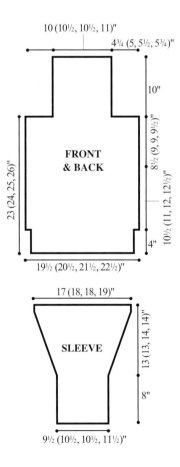

Fashion meets function in Mari Lynn Patrick's ultra-hip pullover and cap. Detachable sleeves make a striking fashion statement; chunky cables and bold ribbed edgings add quick and easy detailing. Shown in size Medium. The Red Pullover and Hat first appeared in the Winter '99/'00 issue of *Vogue Knitting*.

Red Pullover and Hat

VERY EASY VERY VOGUE

SIZES
To fit Small (Medium, Large). Directions are for smallest size with larger sizes in parentheses. If there is only one figure, it applies to all sizes.
Hat
One size fits all

KNITTED MEASUREMENTS
● Bust 47 (49, 51)"/119 (124.5, 129.5)cm
● Length 27½ (28, 28½)"/70 (71, 72.5)cm
● Upper arm 13 (14, 15)"/33 (35, 38)cm

MATERIALS
● 6 (6, 7) 8oz/250g hanks (each approx 310yd/ 279m) of Wool Pak Yarns NZ/Baabajoes Wool Co. *14 Ply* (wool 5) in #01 berry
● One pair each sizes 17 and 19 (12.75 and 16mm) needles
● Cable needle
● Six ⅞"/22mm buttons

GAUGE
10 sts and 13 rows = 6"/15.25cm over St st using larger needles and 3 strands of yarn.
FOR PERFECT FIT, TAKE TIME TO CHECK GAUGE.

Notes
1 Work with 3 strands of yarn held tog throughout.
2 Since changing needle sizes is not an option, just work more tightly or loosely to achieve the gauge.

BACK
With smaller needles and 3 strands of yarn, cast on 43 (45, 47) sts. Work in k1, p1 rib for 4"/10cm. Change to larger needles.
Beg pat Row 1 (RS) P6 (6, 7), k8, p15 (17, 17), k8, p6 (6, 7).
Row 2 K6 (6, 7), p8, k15 (17, 17), p8, k6 (6, 7).
Row 3 Rep row 1.
Row 4 Rep row 2.
Row 5 P6 (6, 7), sl 4 sts to cn and hold to front, k4, k4 from cn (C4L), p15 (17, 17), sl 4 sts to cn and hold to back, k4, k4 from cn (C4R), p6 (6, 7).
Rows 6 and 8 Rep row 2.
Row 7 Rep row 1.
Rep rows 1 to 8 for pat until piece measures 16"/40.5cm from beg. **Next row (RS)** K3, p3 (3, 4), work pat to last 6 (6, 7) sts, p3 (3, 4), k3. **Next row (WS)** P3, k3 (3, 4), work to last 6 (6, 7) sts, k3 (3, 4), p3. Place yarn markers at each side of last row (to mark end of side seams). Cont in pats as established until piece measures 7½" (8, 8½)"/19 (20.5, 21.5)cm from armhole markers.

Shoulder shaping
Note Shoulder shaping is worked in short rows as foll:
Next row (RS) Work to last 3 sts, leave these sts unworked, turn. **Next row (WS)** Sl 1 st, work to last 3 sts, turn.
Next row Sl 1 st, work to last 4 (3, 4) sts, turn. Rep the last row once more.
Next row (RS) Sl 1 st, work to last 4 (5, 5) sts, turn. Rep the last row once more.

Neck shaping
Next row (RS) Sl 1 st, work to center 11 sts, join another 3 strands of yarn and bind off center 11 sts, work to last 4 (5, 5) sts, turn. **Next row (WS)** Sl 1 st, dec 1 st at each neck edge and work to last 4 (5, 5) sts of left shoulder, turn. **Next row (RS)** Bind off all 15 (16, 17) sts of first shoulder, then bind off all 15 (16, 17) sts of 2nd shoulder.

FRONT
Work as for back until piece measures 6½ (7, 7½)"/16.5 (17.5, 19)cm from armhole markers.

Neck shaping
Next row (RS) Work 19 (20, 21) sts, join another 3 strands of yarn and bind off center 5 sts; work to end. Working both sides at once, cont to shape neck binding off 2 sts from each neck edge once, then dec 1 st each side every other row twice, AT SAME TIME, when piece measures 7½ (8, 8½)"/19 (20.5, 21.5)cm from armhole markers, work short row shoulder shaping leaving 3 sts unworked from each shoulder edge 1 (2, 1) time, 4 sts 3 (0, 1) times and 5 sts 0 (2, 2) times.

SLEEVES
With smaller needles and 3 strands of yarn, cast on 17 (17, 19) sts. Work in k1, p1 rib for 4"/10cm. Change to larger needles and cont in St st, inc 1 st each side every 6th row 2 (3, 3) times—21 (23, 25) sts. Work even until piece mea-

sures 17½"/44.5cm from beg. Bind off.

FINISHING

Block pieces to measurements. Sew left
shoulder seam.

Neckband

With smaller needles and 3 strands of
yarn, pick up and k 16 sts from back
neck and 25 sts from front neck—41 sts.
Work in k1, p1 rib for 4½"/11.5cm. Bind
off in rib. Sew right shoulder and turtleneck seam. Sew side seams to armhole
markers. Sew sleeve seams. Sew on 3
buttons to WS of each armhole (so that
buttons are hidden on WS) the first one
at shoulder seam and the other 2 at
1"/2.5cm above underarm seam on front
and back. Button sleeves to inside of
armholes using a corresponding bound-
off st for each button.

HAT

Note

Work with 3 strands of yarn held tog
throughout.

Beg at lower edge with size 17
(12.75mm) needles and 3 strands of
yarn, cast on 40 sts. P1 row on WS.
Row 1 (RS) [K10, p10] twice. **Row 2** K
the knit sts and p the purl sts. Rep these
2 rows twice more—piece measures
3"/7.5cm from beg. Dec row (RS) [K4,
k2tog, k4; p4, p2tog, p4] twice. **Next
row** [K9, p9] twice. **Next row** [K3,
k3tog, k3; p3, p3tog, p3] twice. **Next
row** [K7, p7] twice. **Next row** [K2,
k3tog, k2; p2, p3tog, p2] twice. **Next
row** [K5, p5] twice. **Next row** [K1,
k3tog, k1; p1, p3tog, p1] twice. **Next
row** [K3, p3] twice. **Next row** [K1,
k2tog] 4 times—8 sts. P 1 row, k 1 row,
p 1 row. **Next row** K1, k2tog, k1 [k2tog]
twice—5 sts. **Next row** P2tog, p1,
p2tog. Draw yarn through 3 sts and sew
back seam. Block hat flat lightly.

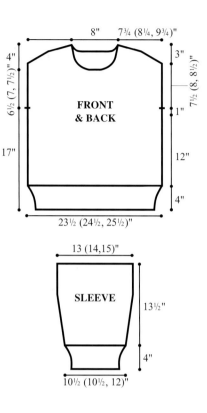

Jumbo stitches and chunky yarns prove that sometimes bigger is better. This extra-bulky turtleneck accentuated with a center cable knits up unbelievably quickly. Shown in size Medium. Designd by Berta Karapetyan, The Chunky Cabled Pullover first appeared in the Winter '00/'01 issue of *Vogue Knitting*.

Chunky Cabled Pullover

VERY EASY VERY VOGUE

SIZES
To fit X-Small/Small (Medium, Large). Directions are for smallest size with larger sizes in parentheses. If there is only one figure, it applies to all sizes.

KNITTED MEASUREMENTS
● Bust 36 (41, 46)"/91.5 (104, 117)cm
● Length 23 (23, 24)"/58.5 (58.5, 61)cm
● Upper arm 14 (14, 15¼)"/35.5 (35.5, 39)cm

MATERIALS
● 9 (9, 11) 3½oz/100g balls (each approx 27yd/25m) of Karabella Yarns *Wool Rope* (wool 6) in #81 natural
● One pair size 36 (20mm) needles OR SIZE TO OBTAIN GAUGE
● Size Q (jumbo crochet hook)
● Cable needle
● Stitch holder

GAUGE
● 5 sts and 8 rows = 6"/15cm over St st using size 36 (20mm) needles.
● 8-st cable panel = 6"/45cm wide.
TAKE TIME TO CHECK GAUGES.

Note
Finished measurements reflect a 1-st selvage taken in at each edge when sewing seams.

BODY
Beg at lower back, cast on 20 (22, 24) sts. **Row 1 (RS)** P6 (7, 8), k8, p6 (7, 8). **Row 2** K6 (7, 8), p8, k6 (7, 8). Rep these 2 rows once more. **Row 5** P6 (7, 8), sl 4 sts to cn and hold to back, k4, k4 from cn (8-st cable), p6 (7, 8). Cont to work in this way, working 8-st cable every 8th row a total of 3 times more, AT SAME TIME, when 8 rows have been completed, work as foll: **Row 9** P1, p2tog, work to last 3 sts, p2tog, p1—18 (20, 22) sts. Work 5 rows even. **Row 15** P1, M1 p-st, work to last st, M1 p-st, p1—20 (22, 24) sts. Work even for 7 rows.

Beg sleeve
Using open cast-on method (with waste yarn), cast on 7 sts at beg of next 2 rows, 6 sts at beg of next 2 rows—46 (48, 50) sts. Work even for 5 (5, 6) more rows.

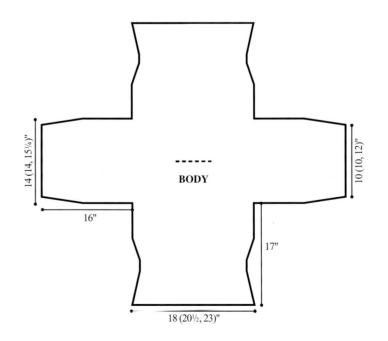

14 (14, 15¼)"

10 (10, 12)"

16"

BODY

18 (20½, 23)"

17"

FRONT

Next row Work 19 (20, 21) sts, sl center 8 sts to holder, using open cast-on method, cast on 8 sts, work to end. Work even in pat reversing cable twist rows and when there are 14 (14, 16) rows total in sleeve, bind off 6 sts at beg of next 2 rows, 7 sts at beg of next 2 rows. Work even for 7 rows. Rep row 9 of back. Work even for 5 rows. Rep row 15. Work even for 8 rows. Bind off.

FINISHING

Block lightly to measurements. Sew side and sleeve seams. With crochet hook, work 1 long sl st in every other row along lower edge of each cuff.

COLLAR
Note

Collar is worked in a tubular knitting technique, working rows straight across. Pick up and k 1 st in side edge of collar. **Row 1** With sts parallel, *sl 1 st from front holder to needle, sl1 st from back holder; rep from * to end, pick up and k 1 st in other side edge of collar—18 sts. Turn. **Next row** *K1, sl 1wyif; rep from * to last st, k last st. Rep last row four times more. Sl odd number sts (sts 1, 3, 5, etc.) to one needle and even number sts (2, 4, 6, etc.) to another needle. Bind off all sts in this order to form circular finish.

Raglan-Sleeve Pullover

Carla Scott uses simple stitch patterns in a palette of autumn shades to create a strikingly simple silhouette. Worked in a variegated yarn, this winter warmer is trimmed with seed-stitch and abalone buttons. Shown in size Medium. The Raglan-Sleeve Pullover first appeared in the Winter '99/'00 issue of *Vogue Knitting*.

VERY EASY VERY VOGUE

Raglan-Sleeve Pullover

SIZES
To fit Small (Medium, Large). Directions are for smallest size with larger sizes in parentheses. If there is only one figure, it applies to all sizes.

KNITTED MEASUREMENTS
● Hip 44 (48, 52, 56, 60)"/111.5 (122, 132, 142, 152.5)cm
● Bust 40 (44, 48, 52, 56)"/101.5 (111.5, 122, 132, 142)cm
● Length 27½ (28, 28½, 29, 29½)"/70 (71, 72.5, 73.5, 75)cm
● Upper arm 15½ (17, 19, 20, 21¾)"/39.5 (43, 48.5, 50.5, 55.5)cm

MATERIALS
● 3 (4, 4, 5, 5) 3½oz/100g balls (each approx 189yd/175m) of Colinette/Unique Kolours *Mohair* (mohair/wool/nylon 4) in #113 velvet leaf (A)
● 2 (2, 3, 3, 3) 3½oz/100g balls (each approx 184yd/166m) of Colinette/Unique Kolours *Wigwam* (cotton 4) in #114 olive (B)
● 4 (4, 5, 5, 6) 3½oz/100g balls (each approx 108yd/100m) of Colinette/Unique Kolours *Isis* (viscose 4) in #113 velvet leaf (C)
● One pair each sizes 9 and 11 (5.5 and 8mm) needles OR SIZE TO OBTAIN GAUGE
● Two novelty buttons

GAUGE
● 12 sts and 24 rows = 4"/10cm over seed st using smaller needles and 1 strand each A and B held tog.
● 9 sts and 16 rows = 4"/10cm over St st using larger needles and 1 strand each A and C held tog.
FOR PERFECT FIT, TAKE TIME TO CHECK GAUGES.

SEED STITCH
Row 1 (RS) *K1, p1; rep from * to end.
Row 2 K the purl sts and p the knit sts.
Rep row 2 for seed st.

BACK
With smaller needles and 1 strand each A and B held tog, cast on 66 (72, 78, 84, 90) sts. Work in seed st for 3"/7.5cm. Cut 1 strand B and join 1 strand C. Change to larger needles. K next row on RS, dec 16 (18, 20, 22, 22) sts evenly spaced across—50 (54, 58, 62, 68) sts. Cont in St st, dec 1 st each side every 5"/12.5cm twice—46 (50, 54, 58, 64) sts. Work even until piece measures 16½"/42cm from beg, end with a WS row.

Raglan armhole shaping
[Dec 1 st each side on next row. Work 1 row even] 8 (11, 14, 15, 18) times. [Dec 1 st each side on next row. Work 3 rows even] 5 (4, 3, 3, 2) times. Bind off rem 20 (20, 20, 22, 24) sts for back neck.

FRONT
Work as for back until there are 22 (22, 22, 24, 26) sts.

Neck shaping
Cont raglan shaping, bind off center 14 sts on next row for neck and working both sides at once, bind off from each neck edge 3 sts once.

SLEEVES
With smaller needles and 1 strand each A and B held tog, cast on 40 (42, 42, 44, 44) sts. Work in seed st for 3"/7.5cm. Cut 1 strand B and join 1 strand C. Change to larger needles. K next row on RS, dec 11 sts evenly spaced across—29 (31, 31, 33, 33) sts. Cont in St st, inc 1 st each side every 14th (10th, 6th, 6th, 4th) row 3 (4, 3, 3, 3) times, every 0 (0, 8th, 8th, 6th) rows 0 (0, 3, 3, 5) times—35 (39, 43, 45, 49) sts. Work even until

piece measures 15"/38cm from beg, end with a WS row.

Raglan cap shaping
Work as for back armhole shaping. Bind off rem 9 sts.

FINISHING
Block pieces to measurements.

Front neckband
With RS facing, smaller needles and 1 strand each A and B held tog, pick up and k 31 (31, 31, 33, 35) sts evenly along front neck. Work in seed st for 2"/5cm. Bind off in pat. Sew raglan sleeve caps to back raglan armholes.

Back neckband
With RS facing, smaller needles and 1 strand each A and B held tog, cast on 7 sts (button flap) pick up and k 38 (38, 38, 40, 42) sts evenly along top of right sleeve, back neck and top of left sleeve, cast on 7 sts (button flap). Work in seed st for 2"/5cm. Bind off in pat. Sew rem raglan sleeve caps to front raglan armholes. With button flap under front neckband, sew a button on each side of neck through both thicknesses. Sew side and sleeve seams.

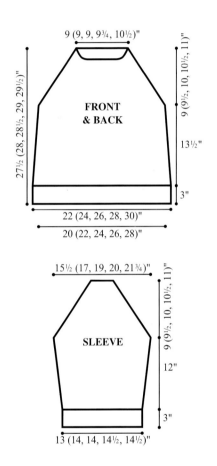

Stitch up a bit of knit whimsy with this drop shoulder pullover designed by Kirsten Cowan. Easy combinations of knit-and-purl and drop stitches create the schoolhouse design; the edges are finished in a single strand of blue. Shown in size Medium. The Schoolhouse Sweater first appeared in the Fall '94 issue of *Vogue Knitting*.

Schoolhouse Sweater

VERY EASY VERY VOGUE

SIZES
To fit Small (Medium, Large). Directions are for smallest size with larger sizes in parentheses. If there is only one figure, it applies to all sizes.

KNITTED MEASUREMENTS
● Bust at underarm 44 (49, 54)"/112 (124.5, 137)cm
● Length 27 (28, 29)"/68.5 (71, 74)cm
● Sleeve width at upper arm 18 (19, 20)"/46 (48.5, 51)cm

MATERIALS
Original Yarn
● 10 (11, 12) 3½oz/100g balls (each approx 100yd/90m) of Cleckheaton/Plymouth *Antarctica* (wool 5) in #1830 sand (MC)
● 1 ball in #1825 teal (A)

Substitute Yarn
● 16 (17, 19) 3¾oz/50g balls (each approx 64yd/59m) of Merino *Supreme* (wool 5) in #2200 cloud
● 2 balls in #2216 blue (A)
● One pair size 10½ (6.5mm) needles OR SIZE TO OBTAIN GAUGE
● Size J/10 (6mm) crochet hook
● Stitch markers

Note
The original yarn used for this sweater is no longer available. A comparable substitute has been made, which is available at the time of printing. Check gauge of substitute yarns very carefully before beginning.

GAUGE
13 sts and 17 rows to 4"/10cm using over St st using size 10½ (6.5mm) needles. FOR PERFECT FIT, TAKE TIME TO CHECK GAUGE.

STITCH GLOSSARY
Double vertical dec: Sl 1 purlwise, p2tog, psso.
Right Purl Twist: K 2nd st, do not sl off needle, p first st, sl both sts from needle.
Left Twist: K 2nd st tbl, do not sl off needle, k first st, sl both sts from needle.
Seed st (any number of sts) **Row 1 (RS)** *K1, p1; rep from *. **Row 2** K the purl sts and p the knit sts. Rep row 2 for seed st pat.
Note
Two selvage sts are included and are not reflected in finished measurements.

BACK
With A, cast on 74 (82, 90) sts. Change to MC. **Row 1 (RS)** K2, *p2, k2; rep from *. Work in k2, p2 rib as established until piece measures 1½"/4cm from beg, end with a RS row. **Next row (WS)** Knit.
Beg chart #1: Row 1 (RS) P1, work 8-st rep 9 (10, 11) times, p1. Working first and last st in rev St st (p on RS, k on WS) for selvage, work chart #1 as established through row 14. **Next row (RS)** Purl. Cont in rev St st until piece measures 18 ¼ (19¼, 20¼)"/46.5 (49, 51.5)cm from beg, end with a WS row.
Beg chart #2: Row 1 (RS) P1, work 8-st rep of chart 9 (10, 11) times, p1. Cont selvage sts in rev St st and work chart #2 as established through row 16.
Beg pat: Row 1 (RS) P1, work seed st pat on 72 (80, 88) sts, p1. Cont selvage

sts and seed st pat as established until piece measures 26½ (27½, 28½)"/67.5 (70, 72.5)cm from beg, end with a WS row.

Neck shaping
Next row (RS) Cont in pat, work 24 (27, 30) sts, join 2nd ball of yarn and bind off center 26 (28, 30) sts, work to end. Working both sides at once, k 1 row. Bind off 24 (27, 30) sts each side. Piece measures 27 (28, 29)"/68.5 (71, 73.5)cm from beg.

FRONT
Work as for back until piece measures 6¼ (6¾, 7¼)"/16 (17.5, 18.5)cm from beg, end with a WS row.
Beg chart #3: Row 1 (RS) P18 (22, 26), pm, work 38 sts of chart #3, pm, p18 (22, 26). Work chart as established through row 47 on sts between markers and work rem sts in rev St st. **Next row (WS)** Knit. Cont in rev St st until piece measures 18¼ (19¼, 20¼)"/46.5 (49, 51.5)cm from beg, end with a WS row. Work chart #2 and seed st pat as for back until piece measures 23 (24, 25)"/58.5 (61, 63.5)cm from beg, end with a WS row.

Neck shaping
Next row (RS) Cont in pat, work 37 (41, 45) sts, join 2nd ball of yarn, work to end. Working both sides at once, dec 1 st at each neck edge every row 13 (14, 15) times—24 (27, 30) sts rem each side. Work even in pat until piece measures same as back to shoulder. Bind off all sts.

SLEEVES

With A, cast on 30 sts. Change to MC. **Row 1 (RS)** P2, *k2, p2; rep from *. Work in k2, p2 rib as established until piece measures 1½"/4cm from beg, end with a WS row. **Next row (RS)** K1, pm, m1, p to last st, m1, pm, k1—32 sts. P 1 row. **Next (inc) row (RS)** K1, m1, work 30 sts in seed st pat, m1, k1—34 sts. Work first and last st in St st for selvage and work 15 rws more in seed st pat, AT SAME TIME, rep inc row (working inc sts into seed st pat) every other row twice, then every 4th row—42 sts. **Next row (RS)** K1, m1, k to last st, m1 k1—44sts. K 1 row.

Beg chart #1: Row 1 (RS) P2, work 8-st rep of chart 5 times, p2. Work pat and incs simultaneously as foll: Work chart #1 as established through row 14, then work all sts in rev St st, AT SAME TIME, inc 1 st each side (working inc sts in rev St st) every 4th row 0 (4, 10) times, every 6th row 5 (5, 1) times, every 8th

row 2 (0, 0) times—58 (62, 66) sts. Work even until piece measures 18"/45.5cm from beg. Bind off all sts.

FINISHING

Block pieces. Sew shoulder seams. With RS facing, crochet hooko and A, work 1 row sc around neck. Place markers 9 (9½, 10)"/23 (24.5, 25.5)cm down from shoulders on front and back for armholes. Sew top of sleeves between markers. Sew side and sleeve seams.

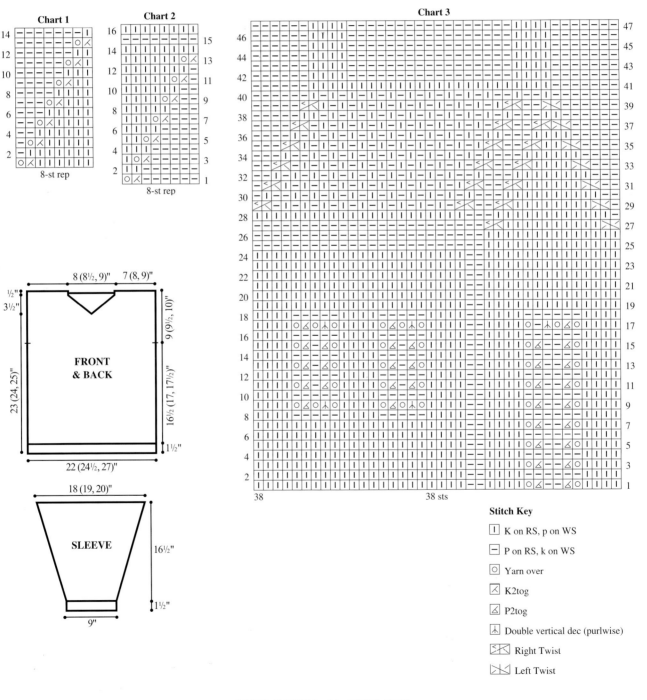

Stitch Key

⊓ K on RS, p on WS

— P on RS, k on WS

○ Yarn over

╱ K2tog

◿ P2tog

⋏ Double vertical dec (purlwise)

⊠ Right Twist

⊠ Left Twist

Snowflake Pullover

Capture the spirit of the winter season with Suzann Thompson's mock-turtleneck snowflake sweater. Relaxed and simple side slits make way for everyday ease. Shown in size Large. The Snowflake Pullover first appeared in the Winter '94/'95 issue of *Vogue Knitting*.

VERY EASY VERY VOGUE

Snowflake Pullover

SIZES
To fit Small (Medium, Large). Directions are for smallest size with larger sizes in parentheses. If there is only one figure, it applies to all sizes.

KNITTED MEASUREMENTS
● Bust at underarm 45 (49, 55)"/ 114.5 (124.5, 139.5)cm
● Length 27 (28, 29)"/68.5 (71, 74)cm
● Sleeve width at upper arm 19 (20, 21)"48.5 (51, 53)cm

MATERIALS
Original Yarn
● 9 (9, 10) 3½oz/100g balls (each approx 55yd/50m) of Adrienne Vittadini *Fabianna* (wool 6) in #80 ecru (A)
● 4 balls in #53 brown (B)
Substitute Yarn
● 6 (6, 7) 3½oz/100g balls (each approx 93yd/85m) of Reynolds/JCA *Allagash* (wool 6) in #657 cream (A)
● 3 balls in #655 toast (B)
● One pair size 15 (10mm) needles OR SIZE TO OBTAIN GAUGE
● Size 11 (8mm) circular needle, 16"/40cm
● Stitch markers

Note
The original yarn used for this sweater is no longer available. A comparable substitute has been made, which is available at the time of printing. Check gauge of substitute yarns very carefully before beginning.

GAUGE
8 sts and 12 rows to 4"/10cm over St st using size 15 (10mm) needles.
FOR PERFECT FIT, TAKE TIME TO CHECK GAUGE.

STITCH GLOSSARY
Rib pat (multiple of 6 sts plus 1 extra)
Row 1 (WS) K2, p3, *k3, p3; rep from *, end k2. **Row 2 (RS)** Knit. Rep rows 1-2 for rib pat.
Stripe pat in St st (k on RS, p on WS), work *2 rows B, 6 rows A; rep from * for stripe pat.

BACK
With larger needles and A, cast on 43 (49, 55) sts. Work 7 rows in rib pat and for size small only, inc 2 sts across last row—45 (49, 55) sts. Cont to work first and last 2 sts in garter st (k every row), beg with a k row and B and work 8 rows in stripe pat. Cont to work first and last 2 sts in garter st and work 2 rows more in stripe pat. Discontinue working 2 sts at each edge in garter st. **Beg chart: Row 1 (RS)** Cont in St st and beg as indicated, work to rep, work 16-st rep twice, end as indicated. Work through chart row 21 as established. Change to B and p 1 row, then k 1 row. Cont in stripe pat as established until piece measures 17 (17½, 18)"/43.5 (44.5, 46)cm from beg, end with a WS row.

Armhole shaping
Cont in pat, bind off 4 sts at beg of next 2 rows—37 (41, 47) sts. Work even until armhole measures 9½ (10, 10½)"/24.5 (25.5, 27)cm, end with a WS row.

Shoulder shaping
Bind off 10 (11, 14) sts at beg of next 2 rows. Bind off rem 17(19, 19) sts. Work as for back until armhole measures 8½ (9, 9½)"/21.5 (23, 24.5)cm, end with a WS row.

Neck shaping
Next row (RS) Work 15 (16, 19) sts, join 2nd ball of yarn and bind off 7 (9, 9) sts, work to end. Working both sides at once, bind off from each neck edge 3 sts once, 2 sts once. Work even and when armhole measures same as back to shoulder, bind off rem 10 (11, 14) sts each side.

SLEEVES
With larger needles and A, cast on 25 sts. Work 7 rows in rib pat, inc 1 st on last row—26 sts. Beg with a k row and B, work in stripe pat, AT SAME TIME, inc 1 st each side (working inc sts into stripe pat) every 4th row 0 (0, 3) times, every 6th row 5 (7, 5) times, every 8th row 1 (0, 0) times—38 (40, 42) sts. Work even until piece measures 17 (17½, 18)"/43.5 (44.5, 46)cm from beg. Bind off all sts.

FINISHING
Sew both shoulder seams.

Highneck
With RS facing, circular needle and A, pick up and k36 (42, 42) sts evenly around neck edge. Place marker, join and work in rnds as foll: **Rnd 1** *P3, k3;

rep from *. **Rnd 2** Knit. Rep rnds 1-2 until highneck measures 2½"/6.5cm from beg. Bind off loosely in pat. Sew straight edge of sleeves to armhole. Sew bound-off body sts to side edges of sleeves. Leaving garter st at lower edges open, sew side and sleeve seams.

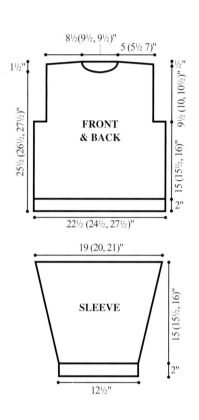

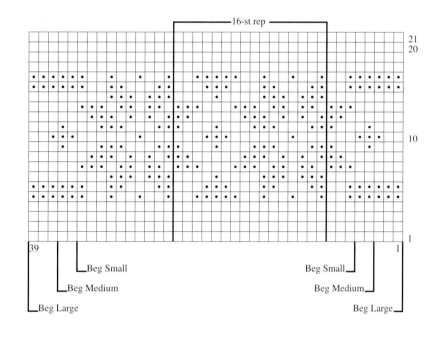

Chic and sophisticated, Margaret Bruzelius's oversized rib-and-cable patterned pullover in hazy mohair embraces maximum comfort and unbeatable charm. Shown in size 36. The Horseshoe Cable Pullover first appeared in the Fall/Winter '87 issue of *Vogue Knitting*.

Horseshoe Cable Pullover

VERY EASY VERY VOGUE

SIZES
To fit 30-32 (34, 36, 38, 40)"/76-81 (86, 91, 96, 101)cm bust. Directions are for smallest size with larger sizes in parentheses. If there is only one set of figures it applies to all sizes.

KNITTED MEASUREMENTS
● Bust 36 (40, 44, 46, 48)"/92 (96, 108, 116, 120)cm
● Length 21½ (22½, 23, 24, 25)"/54.5 (57, 58.5, 61, 63.5)cm
● Sleeve width at upper arm 19 (20, 20, 21, 22)"/48 (51, 51, 53, 56)cm

MATERIALS
Original Yarn
● 15 (16, 17, 18, 20) 1¾oz/50g balls (each approx 60yd/55m) of Vendome *Maurice* (silk/ mohair/wool 5) in #1000 yellow
Substitute Yarn
● 7 (8, 8, 8, 9) 1¾oz/50g balls (each approx 135yd/125m) of Rowan Yarns *Kid Soft* (merino/mohair/nylon 5) in #758 lt. green
● One pair each sizes 9 and 10 (5.5 and 6mm) needles OR SIZE TO OBTAIN GAUGE
● Cable needle (cn)

Note
The original yarn used for this sweater is no longer available. A comparable substitute has been made, which is available at the time of printing. Check gauge of substitute yarns very carefully before beginning.

GAUGE
● 13 sts and 20 rows to 4"/10cm over St st using size 10 (6mm) needles.
● 20 sts and 20 rows to 4"/10cm over rib horseshoe cable using size 10 (6mm) needles.
FOR PERFECT FIT, TAKE TIME TO CHECK GAUGES.

Note
Follow either written or chart instructions for rib horseshoe cable.

STITCH GLOSSARY
Right Cross (over 8 sts): Sl next 4 sts to cn and hold to back, k1, p2, k1; then k1, p2, k1 from cn.
Left Cross (over 8 sts): Sl next 4 sts to cn and hold to front, k1, p2, k1; then k1, p2, k1 from cn.
Rib Horseshoe Cable (20 sts) **Row 1 (RS)** P2, k1, [p2, k2] 3 times, p2, k1, p2. **Row 2** and all WS rows K2, p1, k2, [p2, k2] 3 times, p1, k2. **Row 3** P2, right cross over 8 sts, left cross over 8 sts, p2. **Rows 5, 7 and 9** Rep row 1. **Row 10** Rep row 2. Rep rows 1-10 for rib horseshoe cable.

BACK
With smaller needles, cast on 80 (84, 92, 96, 100) sts.
Beg rib pat: Row 1 (RS) K5 (6, 8, 9, 10), [p2, k1, (p2, k2) 3 times, p2, k1, p2, k5 (6, 8, 9, 10)] 3 times, **Row 2** K the knit sts and p the purl sts. Rep rows 1 and 2 for 1"/2.5cm, end with a row 2. Change to larger needles Beg St st and cable pat; **Row 1 (RS)** K5 (6, 8, 9, 10), [work row 1 of cable over 20 sts, k5 (6, 8, 9, 10)] 3 times. Cont in St st and

cable pat until piece measures 11 (11½, 12, 12½, 13)"/28 (29, 30.5, 32, 33)cm from beg.

Armhole shaping
Bind off 3 (3, 4, 4, 4) sts at beg of next 2 rows—74 (78, 84, 88, 92) sts. Cont in pats, until armhole measures 9½ (10, 10, 10½, 11)"/24 (25.5, 25.5, 26.5, 28)cm.

Shoulder shaping
Bind off 11 (11, 12, 12, 13) at beg of next 2 rows, 11 (12, 12, 13, 13) sts at beg of next 2 rows.

High neck
Cont in pat on 30 (32, 36, 38, 40) sts until high neck measures 4"/10cm from last shoulder bind-off. Bind off all sts loosely.

FRONT
Work as for back.

SLEEVES
With smaller needles, cast on 45 (45, 46, 46, 46) sts.
Beg rib pat: Row 1 (RS) P2, k1, [p2, k2] 3 times, p2, k1, p2, k5 (5, 6, 6, 6), p2, k1, [p2, k2] 3 times, p2, k1, p2. **Row 2** K the knit sts and p the purl sts. Rep rows 1 and 2 for 1"/2.5cm, end with a row 2. Change to larger needles. Beg St st and cable pat: **Row 1 (RS)** Work row 1 of cable over 20 sts, k5 (5, 6, 6, 6), work row 1 of cable over 20 sts. Cont in St st and cable pat, AT SAME TIME, inc 1 st each end (working inc sts into St st) every 4th row 8 (13, 9, 13, 18) times, then every 6th row 7 (4, 7, 5, 2) times—75 (79, 78, 82, 86) sts. Work even until

piece measures 17 (17½, 18, 18½, 19)"/43 (44, 45, 47, 48)cm from beg, end with a WS row. Bind off all sts.

FINISHING

Block pieces. Sew shoulder seams and sides of high neck. Sew top of sleeve to straight edge of armhole, then sew last 1¼"/3cm of sleeve to bound-off sts of front and back armhole. Sew side and sleeve seams.

RIBBED HORSESHOE CABLE

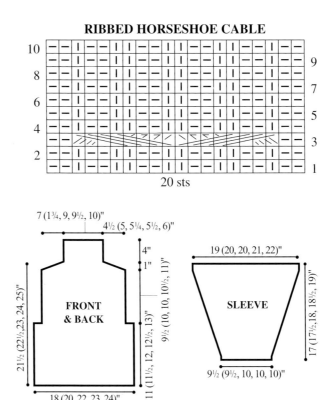

20 sts

Terrific Texture

Warm up to the
hottest looks
on the fashion front—
these knock out knits
boast round-the-clock appeal.

Chunky seed-stitch shows its casual cool in a roomy drop-shoulder cowl-neck pullover. Worked in fiery red wool, this weekend wonder is a breeze to stitch. Show in size Large. The Oversized Seed-Stitch Pullover first appeared in the Winter '95/'96 issue of *Vogue Knitting*.

Oversized Seed-Stitch Pullover

VERY EASY VERY VOGUE

SIZES
To fit X-Small (Small, Medium, Large, X-Large). Directions are for smallest size with larger sizes in parentheses. If there is only one figure, it applies to all sizes.

KNITTED MEASUREMENTS
● Bust 43½ (46½, 50, 54, 58)"/110.5 (118, 127, 137, 147)cm
● Length 27½ (27½, 28, 28, 28½)"/70 (70, 71,71,72.5)cm
● Sleeve width at upperarm 16 (16, 17, 17, 18)"/40.5 (40.5, 43, 43, 45.5)cm

MATERIALS
Original Yarn
● 7 (8, 8, 9, 9) 3½oz/100g balls (each approx 137yd/125m) of Cascade *Iceland* (wool 5) in #253 red (A)
● 6 (7, 7, 8, 8) 1¾oz/50g balls (each approx 164yd/150m) of Cascade *Color Kid* (mohair/acrylic 3) in #148 red (B)
Substitute Yarn
● 11 (13, 13, 14, 14) 1¾oz/50g balls (each approx 88yd/80m) of Filatura Di Crosa/Tahki•Stacy Charles, Inc. *Luna* (wool 5) in #223 red
● 6 (6, 6, 7, 7) 1¾oz/50g balls (each approx 192yd/175m) of Filatura Di Crosa/Tahki•Stacy Charles, Inc. *Butterfly* (mohair/ acrylic 5) in #408 red
● One pair size 15 (10mm) needles OR SIZE TO OBTAIN GAUGE

Note
The original yarn used for this sweater is no longer available. A comparable substitute has been made, which is available at the time of printing. Check gauge of substitute yarns very carefully before beginning.

GAUGE
10 sts and 16 rows to 4"/10 cm over seed st using size 15 (10 mm) needles and 1 strand each A and B held tog. FOR PERFECT FIT, TAKE TIME TO CHECK GAUGE.

SEED STITCH (any number of sts)
Row 1 (RS) *K1, p1; rep from * to end.
Row 2 K the purl sts and p the knit sts. Rep rows 1 and 2 for seed st.

BACK
With size 15 (10 mm) needles and 1 strand each A and B held tog, cast on 54 (58, 62, 68, 72) sts. Work in seed st for 27½ (27½, 28, 28, 28½)"/70 (70, 71, 71, 72.5)cm, end with a WS row. **Next row (RS)** Bind off 13 (15, 16, 19, 21) sts, work 28 (28, 30, 30, 30) sts and place on a holder, bind off rem 13 (15, 16, 19, 21) sts.

FRONT
Work as for back until piece measures 26 (26, 26½, 26½, 27)"/66 (66, 67, 67, 68.5)cm from beg, end with a WS row.

Neck shaping
Next row (RS) Work 18 (20, 21, 24, 26) sts, sl center 18 (18, 20, 20, 20) sts to a holder, join 2nd balls of yam and work to end. Working both sides at once, bind off from each neck edge 3 sts once, 2 sts once. When same length as back, bind off rem 13 (15, 16, 19, 21) sts each side for shoulders.

SLEEVES
With size 15 (10mm) needles and 1 strand each A and B held tog, cast on 26 (26, 26, 26, 27) sts. Work in seed st, inc 1 st each side (working inc sts into pat) every 8th (8th, 8th, 8th, 6th) row 7 (7, 8, 8, 9) times— 40 (40, 42, 42, 45) sts. Work even until piece measures 16½"/42cm from beg. Bind off all sts.

FINISHING
Block pieces to measurements. Sew one shoulder seam.

Collar
With RS facing, size 15 (10mm) needles and 1 strand each A and B held tog, work 28 (28, 30, 30, 30) sts from back neck holder in seed st as established, pick up and k 6 sts along left front neck, work 18 (18, 20, 20, 20) sts from front neck holder in seed st as established, pick up and k 6 sts along right front neck—58 (58, 62, 62, 62) sts. Corn in seed st for 8"/20.5cm. Bind off in pat. Sew 2nd shoulder and collar seam. Place markers 8 (8, 8½, 8½, 9)"/20.5 (20.5, 21.5, 21.5, 23)cm down from shoulder seams on front and back for armholes. Sew top of sleeves between markers. Sew side and sleeve seams.

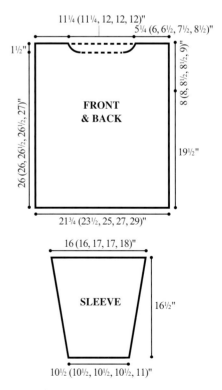

11¼ (11¼, 12, 12, 12)"
5¼ (6, 6½, 7½, 8½)"
1½"
8 (8, 8½, 8½, 9)"
FRONT & BACK
26 (26, 26½, 26½, 27)"
19½"
21¾ (23½, 25, 27, 29)"

16 (16, 17, 17, 18)"
SLEEVE
16½"
10½ (10½, 10½, 10½, 11)"

A center horseshoe cable, garter ridges and relaxed silhouette add up to one knockout knit. Designed by Deborah Newton, this casual style features a shirttail back and face-framing high neck. Show in size Medium. The Relaxed Cable Pullover first appeared in the Fall '94 issue of *Vogue Knitting*.

Relaxed Cable Pullover

VERY EASY VERY VOGUE

SIZES
To fit Small (Medium, Large). Directions are for smallest size with larger sizes in parentheses. If there is only one figure, it applies to all sizes.

KNITTED MEASUREMENTS
● Bust at underarm 44 (48, 52)"/112 (122, 132)cm.
● Length (back) 27 (28, 29)"/68.5 (71, 74)cm.
● Length (front) 23 (24, 25)"/58.5 (61, 63.5)cm.
● Sleeve width at upper arm 17 (18, 19)"/43.5 (46, 48.5)cm.

MATERIALS
Original Yarn
● 14 (15,16) 3½oz/100g balls (each approx 82yd/75m) of Filatura di Crosa/Stacy Charles *Zip* (cotton 5) in #8 camel (MC)
● 1 ball or small amount in #10 pale teal (CC)
Substitute Yarn
● 21 (24, 26) 1¾oz/50g balls (each approx 52yd/48m) of Tahki Yarns *Capri* (cotton 5) in #016 navy (MC)
● 2 balls or small amount #001 white
● One pair each sizes 10½ and 11 (6½ and 8mm) needles OR SIZE TO OBTAIN GAUGE
● Cable needle (cn)
● Stitch markers and holders

Note
The original yarn used for this sweater is no longer available. A comparable substitute has been made, which is available at the time of printing. Check gauge of substitute yarns very carefully before beginning.

GAUGE
● 12 sts and 16 rows to 4"/10cm over St st using size 11 (8mm) needles.
● 16 sts and 16 rows to 4"/10cm over garter horseshoe cable pat using size 11 (8mm) needles.
FOR PERFECT FIT, TAKE TIME TO CHECK GAUGES.

STITCH GLOSSARY
Garter stripe (any number of sts)
Rows 1, 3, 5, 7, 9, 11 (RS) Knit. Rows 2, 4, 6, 8, 10 Purl. Rows 12-16 Knit. Rep rows 1-16 for garter stripe pat.
Garter horseshoe cable (over 16 sts)
Rows 1, 3. 5, 9, 11 (RS) P2, k2, p2, k4, p2, k2, p2. **Rows 2,4, 6, 8,10** K2, p2, k2, p4, k2, p2, k2. **Row 7** P2, sl 4 to cable needle (cn) and hold to back of work, k2, then p2, k2 from cn; sl 2 to cn and hold to front of work, k2, p2, then k2 from cn; p2. **Rows 12-16** Knit. Rep rows 1-16 for cable pat.

BACK
With smaller needles and CC, cast on 70 (76, 82) sts. K 1 row. P 1 row. Change to MC. P 1 row. Change to larger needles.
Beg pats: Row 1 (RS) K3, place marker (pm), work 24 (27, 30) sts in garter stripe pat, 16 sts in garter horseshoe cable pat, 24 (27, 30) sts in garter stripe pat, pm, k3. Working first and last 3 sts in garter st (k every row), cont in pats as established until piece measures 17 (17½, 18)"/43.5 (44.5, 46)cm from beg, end with a WS row.

Armhole shaping
Cont in pat, bind off 3 sts at beg of next 2 rows—64 (70, 76) sts. Work even until armhole measures 8½ (9, 9½)"/21.5 (23, 24.5)cm, end with a WS row.

Shoulder shaping
Bind off 7 (8, 9) sts at beg of next 4 rows, 5 (5, 6) sts at beg of next 2 rows. Sl rem 26 (28, 28) sts to holder.

FRONT
Work as for back until piece measures 13 (13½, 14)"/33 (34.5, 35.5)cm from beg, end with a WS row. Shape armhole as for back. Work even until armhole measures 7½ (8, 8½)"/19 (20.5, 21.5)cm, end with a WS row. Make note of last row of garter horseshoe cable pat worked.

Neck and shoulder shaping
Next row (RS) K24 (27, 30) sts, sl center 16 sts to holder, join 2nd ball of yarn and work to end. Working both sides at once, bind off from each neck edge 2 sts twice, dec 1 st every other row 1 (2, 2) times, AT SAME TIME, when armhole measures same as back to shoulder, shape shoulders as for back.

SLEEVES
With smaller needles and CC, cast on 26 (26, 28) sts. K 1 row. P 1 row. Change to MC. P 1 row. Change to larger needles. **Next row (RS)** Knit. Cont in St st (k on RS, p on WS), AT SAME TIME, inc 1 st each side (working inc sts into St st) every 6th row 5 times, every 8th row 8 (9,10) times—52 (54, 58) sts.

Work even until sleeve measures 18"/46cm from beg. Bind off all sts.

FINISHING
Block pieces lightly. Sew left shoulder seam.

Neckband
With RS facing, smaller needles and MC, pick up and k26 (28, 28) sts from holder, 10 sts from front neck, pm, 16 sts from holder, pm, 10 sts from front neck—62 (64, 64) sts. **Next row (WS)** K to marker, rep last row of garter horseshoe cable pat worked on front, k to end. Work sts before and after markers in garter st and cont garter horseshoe cable pat as established on 16 sts between markers until neckband measures 2"/5cm from beg, end with a WS row. Change to CC. K 2 rows. Bind off all sts. Sew right shoulder seam, including neckband. Sew top of sleeve to straight edge of armhole. Sew bound-off sts of body to side edge of sleeves. Sew side seams, leaving 4½ (5, 5½)"/11.5(13, 14)cm open at lower front edge. Sew sleeve seams.

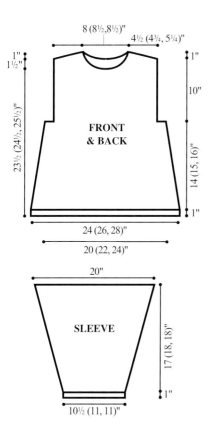

Big stitches, whisper-soft yarn, and classic shaping work together to create this tastefully trendy pullover and cap. Designed by Agi Revesz, the cropped top features cuffed stovepipe sleeves, "mistake-stitch" ribbing and a slight V-neck; the matching ribbed cap is finished with a rolled edge. Shown in size Medium. The Cropped Pullover and Cap first appeared in the Fall '94 issue of *Vogue Knitting*.

Cropped Pullover and Cap

VERY EASY VERY VOGUE

SIZES
To fit Small (Medium, Large). Directions are for smallest size with larger sizes in parentheses. If there is only one figure it applies to all sizes. Hat shown in one size.

KNITTED MEASUREMENTS
- Bust (slightly stretched) 42 (46,51)"/106.5(117, 129.5)cm
- Length 17½ (18, 18½)"/44.5 (46, 47)cm
- Sleeve width at upper arm 13 (14, 14)"/33 (35.5, 35.5)cm

MATERIALS
Pullover:
Original Yarn
- 7 (8, 8) ⅞oz/25g balls (each approx 122yd/112m) of Tiber *New Angora* (angora/ wool/acrylic 4) in #C986 moss (A)
- 5 (5, 6) 1¾oz/50g balls (each approx 153yd/140m) of Tiber *Le Doux Mohair* (mohair/acrylic/ 4) in #C67 sage (B)
- One pair size 11 (8mm) needles OR SIZE TO OBTAIN GAUGE
Hat:
- 1 ⅞oz/25g ball of Tiber's New Angora in #C986 moss (A)
- 1 1¾oz/50g ball of Tiber's Le Doux Mohair in #C67 sage (B)
Substitute Yarn
- 8 (9, 9) ⅞oz/25g balls (each approx 116yd/107m) of Anny Blatt *Angora Super*(angora/ wool 3) in #598 green (A)
- 7 (7, 8) 1¾oz/50g balls (each approx 109yd/100m) of Kid' Anny (mohair/wool 4) in #617 green (A)
Hat:
- 1 ⅞oz/25g ball of Anny Blatt *Angora Super* in #598 green. (A)
- 1 1¾oz/50g balls of *Kid' Anny* in #617 green (A)
- One each sizes 8 and 11 (5 and 8mm) circular needle, 16"/40cm
- One set of four size 11 (8mm) double pointed needles (dpn)

Note
The original yarn used for this sweater is no longer available. A comparable substitute has been made, which is available at the time of printing. Check gauge of substitute yarns very carefully before beginning.

GAUGE
13 sts and 18 rows to 4"/10cm over mistake stitch pat using 1 strand each A and B held tog and size 11 (8mm) needles. FOR PERFECT FIT, TAKE TIME TO CHECK GAUGE.

Mistake stitch pattern
(multiple of 4 sts + 3 extra)
Row 1 *K2, p2; rep from * end k2, p1. Rep row 1 for mistake stitch pat.
Note
Use 1 strand each of A and B held tog.

PULLOVER

BACK
Cast on 67 (75, 83) sts. Work in mistake stitch pat for17½ (18, 18½)"/44.5 (46, 47)cm. Bind off all sts.

FRONT
Work as for back until piece measures 12½ (13, 13½)"/32 (33, 34.5)cm from beg.

Neck shaping
Next row (RS) Work 33 (37, 41) sts, join 2nd balls of yarn and bind off 1 st, work to end.
Next row (WS) Work in pat to last 2 sts, p2tog. On rem side, p2tog, *k2, p2; rep from *, end k2, p1. Cont in pat, working both sides at once, and dec 1 st at each neck edge every row 11 (12, 13) times more. Work even until same length as back. Bind off rem 21 (24, 27) sts each side for shoulders.

SLEEVES
Cast on 35 (39, 39) sts. Work in mistake stitch pat, AT THE SAME TIME, inc 1 st each side (working inc sts into pat) every 18 rows or every 4"/10cm 4 times—43 (47, 47) sts. Work even until piece measures 20 (21, 21)"/51 (53.5, 55.5)cm from beg. Bind off all sts.

FINISHING
Sew left shoulder seam.

V-neck
With RS facing and 1 strand each A and B held tog, pick up 24 (26, 28) sts along back neck, 17 (19, 21) sts along left front neck, place marker, 1 st at center point of V, place marker, 17 (19, 21) sts along right front neck—58 (64, 70) sts.
Row 1 (WS) *K1, p1; rep from * to marker, p1, rep from *; end k1. **Row 2 (RS)** P1, *k1, p1; rep from * to 2 sts before marker, p2tog, k1, p2tog; work to end. Work 1 more row in k1, p1 rib, dec as

before. Bind off loosely. Sew right shoulder seam and neckband. Place markers 6½ (7, 7)"/16.5 (18, 18)cm down from shoulders on front and back. Sew straight edge of sleeve between markers. Sew side and sleeve seams. Fold 3"/7.5cm at lower sleeved edge to RS for cuff and tack in place.

Mistake stitch pat (circularly knit)
(multiple of 4 sts)
Rnd 1 *K2, p2; rep from *. **Rnd 2** K1, "p2, k2; rep from *, end p2, k1. Rep rnds 1-2 for mistake stitch pat.
(Note: Change to dpn when necessary.)
With smaller circular needle and 1 strand each A and B held tog, cast on 64 sts. Place marker and join, being careful not to twist sts. Rnd 1 Knit. Rep rnd 1 until piece measures 2"/5cm from beg, end at marker. Change to larger circular needle. Beg with rnd 1, work mistake-stitch pat for 3"/7.5cm. Cont in pat and work decs as foil: Next (dec) rnd: [K2tog tbl, work 14 sts] 4 times—60 sts. Next (dec) rnd: [K2tog tbl, work 13 sts] 4 times—56 sts. Cont to dec in same way, working 1 st less between decs, until 4 sts rem. Cut yarn, pull end through rem sts and tighten. Fasten off.

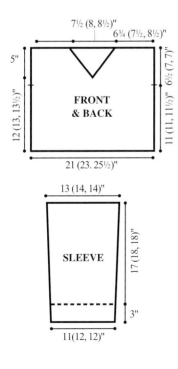

Duplicate-stitched diamonds and big bobbles lend a lighthearted feel to Gitta Schrade's funnelneck pullover. Knit with two strands of yarn held together, it whips up in a flash. Shown in size Medium. The Funnelneck Pullover first appeared in the Winter '00/'01 issue of *Vogue Knitting*.

Funnelneck Pullover

VERY EASY VERY VOGUE

SIZES
To fit X-Small (Small, Medium, Large, X-Large). Directions are for smallest size with larger sizes in parentheses. If there is only one figure, it applies to all sizes.

KNITTED MEASUREMENTS
● Bust 37 (38½, 41½, 44, 49)"/94 (97.5, 105, 111, 124)cm
● Waist 33 (34, 37, 40, 44)"/84 (86, 94, 101.5, 111.5)cm
● Hip 38½ (40, 43, 46, 50)"/98 (101.5, 109, 117, 127)cm
● Length 23½ (24, 24, 24½, 25)"/60 (61, 61, 62.5, 63.5)cm
● Upper arm 12¾ (12¾, 13½, 14, 15)"/32 (32, 34, 35.5, 38)cm

MATERIALS
● 5 (5, 5, 6, 6) 8¾oz/250g hanks (each approx 310yd/284m) of Wool Pak Yarn NZ/Baabajoes Wool Co. *14-Ply* (wool 5) in #17 sky blue (A)
● 1 (1, 1, 1, 2) hanks in #01 natural (B)
● One pair each sizes 10 and 10½ (6 and 6.5mm) needles OR SIZE TO OBTAIN GAUGE
● Size J/9 (6mm) crochet hook
● Stitch holders
● One 1"/25mm button

GAUGE
11 sts and 15 rows = 4"/10cm over St st using larger needles and 2 strands of yarn. FOR PERFECT FIT, TAKE TIME TO CHECK GAUGE.

Note
Work with 2 strands of A held tog throughout. Foll charts for duplicate sts in B and work crochet bobbles after pieces are knit.

BACK
With smaller needles and 2 strands of A held tog, cast on 53 (55, 59, 63, 69) sts. K 3 rows. Change to larger needles and cont in St st until piece measures 4¾ (5¼, 5¼, 5¾, 6¼)"/12 (14, 14, 14.5, 16)cm from beg. Dec 1 st each side of next row then every 6th row 3 times more—45 (47, 51, 55, 61) sts. Work even for 4 rows. Inc 1 st each side of next row then every 4th row twice more—51 (53, 57, 61, 67) sts. Work even until piece measures 15½ (16, 15½, 15½,16)"/39.5 (40.5, 39.5, 39.5, 40.5)cm from beg.

Armhole shaping
Bind off 2 (2, 2, 3, 4) sts at beg of next 2 rows. Dec 1 st each side every other row 1 (1, 2, 2, 3) times, then every 4th row twice—41 (43, 45, 47, 49) sts. Work even until armhole measures 8 (8, 8½, 9, 9)"/20.5 (20.5, 21.5, 23, 23)cm.

Neck and shoulder shaping
Bind off 10 (10, 11, 12, 13) sts at beg of next 2 rows for shoulders. Sl center 21 (23, 23, 23, 23) sts to a holder for neck.

FRONT
Work as for back.

SLEEVES
With smaller needles and 2 strands of A held tog, cast on 25 (25, 27, 27, 29) sts.

K 3 rows. Change to larger needles and cont in St st, inc 1 st each side every 10th row 5 (5, 5, 6, 6) times—35 (35, 37, 39, 41) sts. Work even until piece measures 17½"/44.5cm from beg.

Cap shaping
Bind off 2 (2, 2, 3, 4) sts at beg of next 2 rows. Dec 1 st each side every other row 6 (6, 7, 6, 6) times, every 4th row 1 (1, 1, 2, 2) times. Bind off 3 sts at beg of next 2 rows. Bind off rem 11 sts.

FINISHING
Block pieces to measurements. Sew left shoulder seams.

Collar
With smaller needles and 2 strands of A held tog, cast on 4 sts, then k sts from front and back shoulders—46 (50, 50, 50, 50) sts. Cont in St st for 2"/5cm.
Next row (RS) K to last 4 sts, bind off 2 sts (buttonhole), k to end. P 1 row, casting on 2 sts over bound-off sts of previous row. K 1 row, p 1 row, then p 2 rows. Bind off purlwise. Sew other shoulder seam. Sew on buttons. Centering chart as in photo and beg at lower front edge, with 2 strands of B, work duplicate st (each duplicate st covers 2 rows) over entire front. Rep for back. Work chart on sleeves in same way.

Bobbles
Working in center of front diamonds only, work as foll: with double strand of B, [insert crochet hook from side under center st, pull yarn through, yo] 4 times, pull last yo through all lps on hook, ch 1

to secure. Pull ends to WS and knot in place. Sew sleeves into armholes. Sew side and sleeve seams.

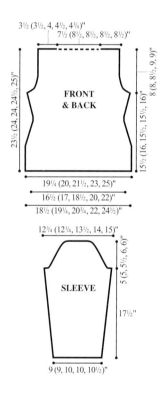

Front & Back

Color Key
- ☐ MC
- Ⅴ Duplicate st with CC
- • Bobble with CC

Sleeve

3½ (3½, 4, 4½, 4¾)"
7½ (8½, 8½, 8½, 8½)"

8 (8, 8½, 9, 9)"

FRONT & BACK

23½ (24, 24, 24½, 25)"

15½ (16, 15½, 15½, 16)"

19¼ (20, 21½, 23, 25)"
16½ (17, 18½, 20, 22)"
18½ (19¼, 20¾, 22, 24½)"

12¾ (12¾, 13½, 14, 15)"

5 (5, 5½, 6, 6)"

SLEEVE

17½"

9 (9, 10, 10, 10½)"

Billowy soft mohair showcases high-impact stitchery. Deborah Newton uses chunky mohair and bold basketweave stitches to spark up a classic dropped-shoulder silhouette. Show in size Medium. The Mohair Basketweave Pullover first appeared in the Winter '94 issue of *Vogue Knitting*.

Mohair Basketweave Pullover

VERY EASY VERY VOGUE

SIZES
To fit Small (Medium, Large). Directions are for smallest size with larger sizes in parentheses. If there is only one figure it applies to all sizes.

KNITTED MEASUREMENTS
● Bust 43 (46, 50)"/106.5 (117, 127)cm
● Length 19 (20, 21)"/48 (51, 53.5)cm
● Sleeve width at upper arm 18 (18½, 20)"/46 (47, 51)cm

MATERIALS
Original Yarn
● 8 (9, 11) 8oz/228g balls (each approx 101yd/92m) Classic Elite Yarns *Mountain Home Mohair-Heavy* (mohair 6) in #5205 ecru
Substitute Yarn
● 9 (10, 12) 1½oz/40g balls (each approx 90yd/92m) Classic Elite Yarns *La Gran* (mohair/wool/nylon 4) in #6516 natural
● One pair size 10½ (6.5mm) needles, OR SIZE TO OBTAIN GAUGE
● Size 10½ (6.5mm) circular needle 16"/40cm
● Strong plied wool in matching color for sewing seams

Note
The original yarn used for this sweater is no longer available. A comparable substitute has been made, which is available at the time of printing. Check gauge of substitute yarns very carefully before beginning.

GAUGE
12 sts and 18 rows to 4"/10cm over basketweave pat using size 10½ (6.5mm) needles.
FOR PERFECT FIT, TAKE TIME TO CHECK GAUGE.

Note
Work with 2 strands held tog.

STITCH GLOSSARY
Rib pat (multiple of 6 sts)
Row 1 (WS) P2, k2, *p4, k2; rep from *, end p2. **Row 2 (RS)** K2, p2, *k4, p2; rep from *, end k2. Rep rows 1-2 for rib pat.
Basketweave pat
(multiple of 6 sts + 2 extra)
Rows 1 and 7 (RS) Knit Rows 2 and 8 (WS) Purl. **Rows 3 and 5 (RS)** K2, *p4, k2; rep from *. **Rows 4 and 6 (WS)** P2, *k4, p2; rep from *. **Rows 9 and 11 (RS)** P3, k2, p4; rep from *, end p3. **Rows 10 and 12 (WS)** K3, *p2, k4; rep from *, end k3. Rep rows 1-12 for basketweave pat.

BACK
Cast on 66 (72, 78) sts. Work even in rib pat for 8"/20.5cm, end with a RS row.
Next row (WS) P2tog, work rib pat to last 2 sts, p2tog—64 (70, 76) sts.
Beg basketweave pat: Next row (RS) K1 (selvage), work row 1 of basketweave pat over next 62 (68, 74) sts, end k1 (selvage). Work even in pat as established, keeping selvage sts in St st, until piece measures 18 (19, 20)"/45.5 (48, 51)cm from beg, end with a WS row.

Neck and shoulder shaping
Cont in pat, bind off 7 (8, 8) sts at beg of next 4 rows, 7 (7, 9) sts at beg of next 2 rows, AT SAME TIME, bind off center 10 (12, 14) sts, and working both sides at once, bind off from each neck edge 3 sts twice.

FRONT
Work as for back until piece measures 17 (18, 19)"/43 (45.5, 48)cm from beg, end with a WS row.

Neck shaping
Next row (RS) Cont in pat, work 27 (29, 31) sts, join 2nd ball of yarn and bind off next 10 (12, 14) sts, work to end. Working both sides at once, bind off from each neck edge 2 sts 3 times—21 (23, 25) sts rem each side, AT SAME TIME, when piece measures same as back to shoulder, shape shoulder as for back.

SLEEVE
Cast on 30 (30, 36) sts. P 1 row. **Next row (RS)** K2 (selvage sts), work row 1 of basketweave pat over next 26 (26, 32) sts, k2 (selvage sts). Work even in pats as established for 3 more rows, keeping selvage sts in St st. **Next (inc) row (RS)** K2, m1, work as established to last 2 sts, m1, k2. Keeping selvage sts in St st and working inc sts into basketweave pat, rep inc row every 6th row 9 times, every 4th row 2 (3, 2) times—54 (56, 60)

sts. Work even until piece measures approx 19"/48cm from beg, end with row 2 or 8 of basketweave pat. Bind off on next row.

FINISHING
Block pieces by steaming lightly on WS if necessary. Sew shoulder seams.

Neckband
With circular needle, RS facing, beg at right shoulder seam and pick up and knit 60 (66, 72) sts around neck edge. Place marker and join. Rnd 1 *P2, k4; rep from *. Rep rnd 1 until neckband measures 5"/12.5cm. Bind off loosely. Place markers 9 (9¼, 10)"/23 (23.5, 25.5)cm down from shoulders on front and back for armholes. Sew top of sleeves between markers. Sew side and sleeve seams.

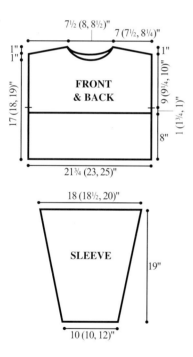

Plush chenille ridges create a striking surface design on Patricia Brown's crimson pullover and cap set. A flattering funnel neck and knuckle-brushing sleeves add to the lean silhouette. Shown in size Small. The Chenille Pullover and Cap first appeared in the Fall '94 issue of *Vogue Knitting*.

Chenille Pullover and Cap

VERY EASY VERY VOGUE

SIZES
To fit Small (Medium, Large). Directions are for smallest size with larger sizes in parentheses. If there is only one figure it applies to all sizes.

KNITTED MEASUREMENTS
Pullover:
● Bust 38½ (41½, 46)"/98 (105.5, 117)cm
● Length (without neck) 24 (25½, 27)"/61 (65, 68.5)cm
● Sleeve width at upper arm 12 (13, 14)"/30.5(33,35.5)cm
Hat:
● Circumference approx 20"/51cm

MATERIALS
Original Yarn
Pullover:
● 4 (4, 5) 1¾oz/50g balls (each approx 165yd/150m) of Trendsetter *Cashmore* (wool/microfiber 3) in #915 wine (A)
● 11 (11, 12) 1¾oz/50g balls (each approx 66yd/60m) of Trendsetter *Canyon* (rayon wool/acrylic 5) in #3396 burgundy (MC)
● One each size 7 (4.5mm) circular needle, 24"/60cm and 16"/40cm, OR SIZE TO OBTAIN GAUGE
● Stitch markers
Hat:
● 1 ball Trendsetter's *Cashmore* in #915 (A)
● 1 ball Trendsetter's *Canyon* in #3396 burgundy (MC)
● Size 7 circular needle, 16"/40cm

Substitute Yarn
Pullover:
● 5 (5, 6) 3½oz/100g balls (each approx 151yd/140m) of Rowan Yarns *Chunky Cotton Chenille* (cotton 5) in #38 red (A)
● 5 (5, 6) 3½oz/100g balls (each approx 151yd/140m) of Magpie *Aran* (wool 5) in #319 red (MC)
Hat:
● 1 ball Rowan Yarns *Chunky Cotton Chenille* in #38 red (A)
● 1 ball Magpie *Aran* in #319 red (MC)
Both:
● One set of four size 7 (4.5mm) double pointed needles (dpn)

Note
The original yarn used for this sweater is no longer available. A comparable substitute has been made, which is available at the time of printing. Check gauge of substitute yarns very carefully before beginning.

GAUGE
Pullover and hat:
15 sts to 4"/10cm and 10 rnds to 1¾"/4.5cm over St st knit circularly using MC and size 7 (4.5mm) needles.
To work gauge swatch:
Cast on 30 sts evenly divided over 3 dpn. K 20 rnds.
FOR PERFECT FIT, TAKE TIME TO CHECK GAUGE.

PULLOVER
Note
1 Body and sleeves are each knit circularly to underarm, then joined to circularly knit yoke. **2** Use 2 strands A held tog. **3** Keep careful count of rnds.

BODY
With MC and longer circular needle, cast on 144 (156, 172) sts. Place marker and join, being careful not to twist sts. Work in rnds as foll: ***With MC, k 1 rnd, then p 8 (10, 10) rnds. With A, k 4 rnds A. **With MC, k 1 rnd, then p 9 (10, 11) rnds. With A, k 4 rnds. Rep from * once. "With MC, k 1 rnd, then p 8 (9, 10) rnds. With A, k 4 rnds. Rep from ** once. With MC, k 1 rnd, then p 8 (8, 9) rnds. With A, k 4 rnds. With MC, k 1 rnd, then p 8 (8, 9) rnds. With A, k 2 rnds, ending at joining marker.*** Mark st immediately after joining marker. Sl all sts to spare needle or holders.

SLEEVES
Note
Change to shorter circular needles when possible.
With MC, cast on 35 (37, 39) sts divided evenly on 3 dpn. Place marker and join, being careful not to twist sts. Work pat and incs simultaneously as foll: Work in rnds as for body between ***'s, AT SAME TIME, inc 1 st at marker every 7th rnd 0 (4, 14) times, every 8th rnd 4 (8, 0) times, every 9th rnd 6 (0, 0) times—45 (49, 53) sts. Sl sts to holder or spare needle.

YOKE
Note
1 Read through instructions as pat and decs are worked simultaneously. **2** Work decs by k2tog before markers and ssk after markers.)

Joining rnd With RS facing, longer circular needle and A, beg with marked st on body and k1, place marker (pm), k70 (76, 84) sts from body (back), pm, k1 from body, pm, k45 (49, 53) sts of 1 sleeve, pm, k1 from body, pm, k70 (76, 84) sts from body (front), pm, k last st from body, pm, k45 (49, 53) sts of 2nd sleeve, pm, and join—234 (254, 278) sts. Working single st between markers as a knit st every rnd, work pat and decs simultaneously as foll: K 1 rnd A; k 1 rnd MC, p 7 (8, 8) rnds MC; k 3 (4, 4) rnds A; k 1 rnd MC, p 7 (7, 8) rnds MC; k 3 rnds A; k 1 rnd MC, p 7 rnds MC; k 3 rnds A; k 1 rnd MC, p 6 (6, 7) rnds MC; k 3 rnds A; k 1 rnd MC, p 5 (6, 6) rnds MC. AT SAME TIME, on front and back, dec 1 st each side at markers every rnd 2 (3, 7) times, every other rnd 24 (25, 24) times; on sleeves, dec 1 st each side at markers every other rnd 1 (4, 8) times, every 3rd rnd 16 (15, 13) times—62 (66, 70) sts.

Funnel neck

With A, k 3 rnds. With MC, k 1 rnd, then p 4 (5, 5) rnds. With A, k 2 rnds. With MC, k 1 rnd, p 4 rnds. With A, k 2 rnds. With MC, k 1 rnd, p 3 rnds. Bind off loosely purlwise.

HAT
Notes
1 Use 2 strands of A held tog.
2 Change to dpn when necessary. With shorter circular needle and MC, cast on 72 sts. Place marker and join, taking care not to twist sts. **Rnd 1** Knit. Rep rnd 1 for 1"/2.5cm. P 8 rnds. **Next rnd** With A, [k16, k2tog] 4 times—68 sts. K 3 rnds. With MC, p 6 rnds. With A, k 1 rnd. **Next rnd** With A, [k15, k2tog] 4 times—64 sts. **Next rnd** [k14, k2tog] 4 times—60 sts. **Next rnd** [K13, k2tog] 4 times—56 sts. **Next rnd** With MC, [p12, p2tog] 4 times—52 sts. In same way, cont to dec 4 sts on next 5 rnds—32 sts. Change to A. K next 4 rnds, dec every other rnd as established—24 sts. Change to MC. P 6 rnds, dec every other rnd 3 times—12 sts. **Next rnd** [P2tog] 6 times—6 sts. **Next rnd** [P2tog] 3 times—3 sts. P 1 rnd. Cut yarn, draw through rem sts, tighten and secure.

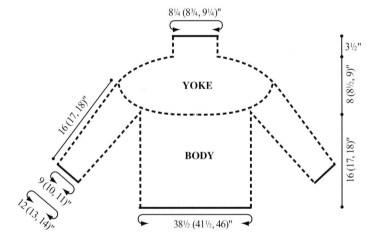

Chic Coverups

Bundling up has never looked so modern. Fashion meets function in textured stitches, cutting edge style and no-fuss shaping to create compelling looks.

Carla Scott's shawl-collared jacket works all season long for maximum warmth and comfort. It knits up fast in easy garter stitch and is accented with patch pockets and a tie belt. Shown in size Small. The Belted Jacket first appeared in the Fall '99 issue of *Vogue Knitting*.

Belted Jacket

VERY EASY VERY VOGUE

SIZES
To fit Small (Medium, Large, X-Large, XX-Large). Directions are for smallest size with larger sizes in parentheses. If there is only one figure, it applies to all sizes.

KNITTED MEASUREMENTS
● Bust (closed) 42 (45, 48, 51, 54)"/106.5 (114.5, 122, 129.5, 137)cm
● Length 26 (26½, 27, 28½, 29)"/66 (67.5, 69, 72.5, 73.5)cm
● Upper arm 14 (15, 16, 18, 19)"/35.5 (38, 40.5, 45.5, 48)cm

MATERIALS
Original Yarn
● 22 (24, 26, 30, 32) 1¾oz/50g balls (each approx 88yd/80m) of Shepherd/Classic Elite Yarns *Aran 12 Ply* (wool/acrylic/viscose 4) in #0431 cinnabar
Substitute Yarn
● 19 (20, 21, 25, 27) 1¾oz/50g balls (each approx 108yd/100m) of Plymouth/Cleckheaton Yarn *Country 8 ply Naturals* (wool/acrylic/viscose 4) in #1823 red
● One pair size 11 (8mm) needles OR SIZE TO OBTAIN GAUGE
● Size K/10½ (7mm) crochet hook

Note
The original yarn used for this sweater is no longer available. A comparable substitute has been made, which is available at the time of printing. Check gauge of substitute yarns very carefully before beginning.

GAUGE
12 sts and 18 rows = 4"/10cm over rev St st using 2 strands of yarn and size 11 (8mm) needles.
TAKE TIME TO CHECK GAUGE.

Note
Work with 2 strands held tog throughout.

BACK
With 2 strands held tog, cast on 64 (68, 73, 77, 82) sts. Work in garter st for 2"/5cm. Cont in rev St st, dec 1 st each side every 8th row 4 times—56 (60, 65, 69, 74) sts. Inc 1 st each side every 8th row 4 times— 64 (68, 73, 77, 82) sts. Work even until piece measures 17½ (17½, 17½, 18, 18)"/44.5 (44.5, 44.5, 45.5, 45.5)cm from beg, end with a WS row.

Armhole shaping
Bind off 3 sts at beg of next 2 rows, 2 sts at beg of next 2 rows. Dec 1 st each side every other row 7 (7, 7, 8, 8) times—40 (44, 49, 51, 56) sts. Work even until armhole measures 7 (7½, 8, 9, 9½)"/17.5 (19, 20.5, 23, 24)cm.

Shoulder shaping
Bind off 3 (4, 5, 5, 6) sts at beg of next 4 rows, 4 (4, 4, 5, 5) sts at beg of next 2 rows. Bind off rem 20 (20, 21, 21, 22) sts for back neck.

LEFT FRONT
With 2 strands held tog, cast on 41 (43, 45, 47, 50) sts. Work in garter st for 2"/5cm.
Next row (RS) P to last 2 sts, k1, p1.
Next row K1, p1, k to end. Cont in pat as established, keeping 2 sts at front edge in k1, p1 rib and rem sts in rev St st, AT SAME TIME, work decs and incs at side edge (beg of RS rows) as for back. Work even until piece measures 15 (15½, 16, 17, 17½)"/38 (39.5, 41, 43.5, 44.5)cm from beg, end with a WS row.
Neck, armhole and shoulder shaping
Dec 1 st at neck edge (end of RS rows) on next row, then every other row 14 (14, 14, 14, 15) times more, then every 4th row 4 times, AT SAME TIME, when same length as back to armhole, shape armhole at side edge same as back, and when same length as back to shoulder, shape shoulder at side edge as for back.

RIGHT FRONT
Work to correspond to left front, reversing shaping and working rib at front edge as foll: **Next row (RS)** P1, k1, p to end. **Next row** K to last 2 sts, p1, k1.

SLEEVES
With 2 strands held tog, cast on 30 (31, 32, 32, 33) sts. Work in garter st for 2"/5cm. Cont in rev St st, inc 1 st each side every 10th (8th, 6th, 4th,4th) row 6 (5, 2, 3, 6) times, every 0 (10th, 8th, 6th, 6th) row 0 (2, 6, 8, 6) times—42 (45, 48, 54, 57) sts. Work even until piece measures 17"/43cm from beg.

Cap shaping
Bind off 3 sts at beg of next 2 rows, 2

sts at beg of next 2 (2, 4, 4, 4) rows, dec 1 st each side every other row 8 (9, 10, 11, 12) times, bind off 2 sts at beg of next 2 (2, 2, 4, 4) rows. Bind off rem 12 (13, 10, 10, 11) sts.

POCKETS
(make 2)
Cast on 16 sts and work in rev St st for 3½"/9cm. Cont in garter st for 1"/2.5cm. Bind off.

FINISHING
Block pieces to measurements. Sew pockets to fronts, at ½"/1.5cm above garter st and 4"/10cm from front edge. Sew shoulder seams.

Collar
With RS facing, beg at right front neck, pick up and k 96 (96, 98, 100, 102) sts evenly along right front, back and left front neck. K 1 row. Cont in garter st, binding off 4 sts at beg of next 20 rows. Bind off rem 16 (16, 18, 20, 22) sts. Set in sleeves. Sew side and sleeve seams. With RS facing and crochet hook, work 1 row sc and 1 row backwards sc (from left to right) evenly around each front edge. Fold collar to RS and work crochet edging in same way around collar. Tack ends of collar at front edges.

Belt
With 2 strands held tog, cast on 5 sts and work in garter st for 65"/165cm. Bind off.

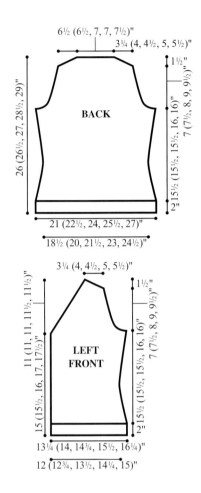

Classic Twin Set

Viola Carol's pretty cardigan-and-shell combo blends fuss-free styling with year-round comfort. Worked in simple stockinette and accented with garter stitch at the collar and cuffs, this all-season staple works up in a flash. Shown in size Small. The Classic Twin Set first appeared in the Fall '99 issue of *Vogue Knitting*.

VERY EASY VERY VOGUE

Classic Twin Set

FOR PERFECT FIT, TAKE TIME TO CHECK GAUGE.

SIZES
To fit Small (Medium, Large). Directions are for smallest size with larger sizes in parentheses. If there is only one figure, it applies to all sizes.

KNITTED MEASUREMENTS
Cardigan
● Bust 36 (38, 40)"/91.5 (96.5, 101.5)cm
● Length 20½ (21½, 22½)"/52 (54.5, 57)cm
● Upper arm 12½ (13½, 15)"/32 (33, 38)cm
Shell
● Bust 32 (34, 36)"/81 (86, 91.5)cm
● Length 18½ (19½, 20½)"/47 (50, 52)cm

MATERIALS
● 5 (6, 7) 3½oz/100g skeins (each approx 245yd/224m of Brown Sheep Co. *Naturespun Worsted* (wool 3) in #113 blue
● One pair each sizes 7 and 8 (4.5 and 5mm) needles OR SIZE TO OBTAIN GAUGE
● Three 1"/25mm novelty buttons

GAUGE
16 sts and 22 rows = 4"/10cm over twisted St st using larger needles.

CARDIGAN

BACK
With smaller needles, cast on 72 (76, 80) sts. Work in garter st for 6 rows. Change to larger needles. **Row 1 (RS)** *K1 tbl; rep from * to end. **Row 2** Purl. Rep these 2 rows for twisted St st until piece measures 13 (13½, 14)"/33 (34, 35.5)cm from beg.

Armhole shaping
Bind off 5 sts at beg of next 2 rows, dec 1 st each side every other row twice—58 (62, 66) sts. Work even until armhole measures 7 (7½, 8)"/18 (19, 20.5)cm.

Neck and shoulder shaping
Next row (RS) Work 19 (20, 21) sts, join 2nd ball of yarn and bind off center 20 (22, 24) sts, work to end. Working both sides at once, bind off 2 sts from each neck edge once. Work even, if necessary, until armhole measures 7½ (8, 8½)"/19 (20.5, 21.5)cm. Bind off rem 17 (18, 19) sts each side for shoulders.

LEFT FRONT
With smaller needles, cast on 40 (42, 44) sts. Work in garter st for 6 rows. Change to larger needles and cont in twisted St st until piece measures 13 (13½, 14)"/33 (34, 35.5)cm from beg.

Armhole shaping
Bind off 5 sts at beg of next RS row (armhole edge), then dec 1 st from arm-hole every other row twice—33 (35, 37) sts. Work even until armhole measures 5½ (6, 6½)"/14 (15, 16.5)cm, end with a RS row.

Neck shaping
Next row (WS) Bind off 6 (7, 7) sts at beg of row, work to end. Cont to bind off 5 (5, 6) sts from neck edge once, 3 sts once and 2 sts once—17 (18, 19) sts. When same length as back, bind off rem sts for shoulders. Place markers for 3 buttons, the first one at 4"/10cm from lower edge, the others spaced at 5½ (6, 6½)"/14 (15, 16.5)cm intervals.

RIGHT FRONT
Work to correspond to left front, reversing shaping and working 3 buttonholes opposite marker as foll: Buttonhole row (RS) Work 4 sts, yo, k2tog for buttonhole, work to end.

SLEEVES
With smaller needles, cast on 40 (42, 44) sts. Work in garter st for 2"/5cm. Change to larger needles and p next row on WS, inc 1 st each side—42 (44, 46) sts. Cont in twisted St st, inc 1 st each side every 14th (12th, 8th) row 4 (5, 7) times—50 (54, 60) sts. Work even until piece measures 15½"/39.5cm from beg.

Cap shaping
Bind off 5 sts at beg of next 2 rows. Dec 1 st each side of next row, then every other row 10 (12, 15) times more. Bind off 2 sts at beg of next 6 rows. Bind off rem 6 sts.

FINISHING

Block pieces to measurements. Sew shoulder seams.

Collar

With smaller needles, pick up and k 58 (62, 66) sts around neck, beg and end at 6 sts from each edge. Work in garter st for 3"/7.5cm. Bind off.

Pockets (make 2)

With smaller needles, cast on 20 sts. Work in garter st for 3"/7.5cm. Bind off. Set sleeves into armholes. Sew side and sleeve seams. Sew on buttons. Sew on pockets at 2"/5cm from lower edge and 2½"/6.5cm from center front.

SHELL

BACK

With smaller needles, cast on 68 (72, 76) sts. Work in garter st for 6 rows. Change to larger needles and cont in twisted St st (see cardigan back) until piece measures 2½ (3, 3½)"/6.5 (7.5, 9)cm from beg. Dec row (RS) Work 14 (16, 18) sts, pm, SKP, k36, pm, k2tog, work 14 (16, 18) sts. P 1 row. **Next row (RS)** Work to first marker, SKP, work to 2nd marker, k2tog, work to end. Rep last 2 rows 3 times more—58 (62, 66) sts. Work even until piece measures 6 (6½, 7)"/15 (16.5, 18)cm from beg. Inc row (RS) K1 tbl, M1, work to last st, M1, k1 tbl. Rep inc row every 8th row twice more—64 (68, 72) sts. Work even until piece measures 12 (12½, 13)"/30.5 (32, 33)cm from beg.

Armhole shaping

Bind off 6 sts at beg of next 2 rows. Dec 1 st each side every other row 1 (2, 2) times—50 (52, 56) sts. Work even until armhole measures 5½ (6, 6½)"/14 (15, 16.5)cm.

Neck shaping

Next row (RS) Work 18 (18, 20) sts, join 2nd ball of yarn and bind off center 14 (16, 16) sts, work to end. Working both sides at once, bind off 3 sts from each neck edge twice. When armhole measures 6½ (7, 7½)"/16.5 (18, 19)cm, bind off rem 12 (12, 14) sts each side for shoulders.

FRONT

Work as for back until armhole measures 4½ (5, 5½)"/11.5 (12.5, 14)cm.

Neck shaping

Next row (RS) Work 18 (18, 20) sts, join 2nd ball of yarn and bind off center 14 (16, 16) sts, work to end. Working both sides at once, bind off 2 sts from each neck edge every other row twice, dec 1 st every other row twice. When same length as back, bind off rem 12 (12, 14) sts each side for shoulders.

FINISHING

Block pieces to measurements. Sew one shoulder seam.

Neckband

With smaller needles, pick up and k 75 (79, 79) sts evenly along neck edge. Work in garter st for 6 rows. Bind off. Sew other shoulder, neckband and side seams.

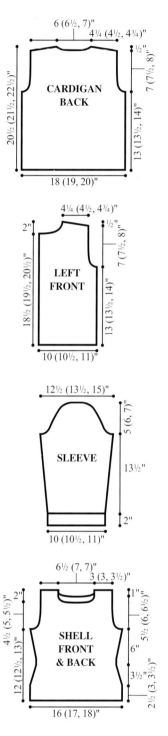

Teva Durham's poncho keeps the shaping simple—let the yarn do the work. A perfect beginner's project, this quick cover up is knit side-to-side in a plush chenille bouclé. One size fits all. The No-Fuss Poncho first appeared in the Winter '99/'00 issue of *Vogue Knitting*.

No-Fuss Poncho

VERY EASY VERY VOGUE

SIZES
One size fits all.

KNITTED MEASUREMENTS
● Length 25"/63.5cm
● Width (sleeve to sleeve edge) 60"/153cm

MATERIALS
● 19 1¾oz/50g balls (each approx 48yd/45m) of Schulana/Skacel Collection *Fiumo* (acrylic/acetate 4) in #2182 fuchsia
● Size 11 (8mm) circular needle, 29"/75cm long OR SIZE TO OBTAIN GAUGE
● Size J/10 (6mm) crochet hook
● Stitch markers

GAUGE
8 sts and 10 rows = 4"/10cm over St st using size 11 (8mm) needles.
TAKE TIME TO CHECK GAUGE.

Note
Poncho is knit from left sleeve edge to right sleeve edge.

BODY
Cast on 100 sts. Working back and forth in rows, work in St st until piece measures 25½"/65cm from beg, end with a WS row.

Beg neck opening
Next row (RS) K50 (back), join a 2nd ball of yarn and k2, k2tog, k to end (front). Work both sides separately for 1 row. Rep neck dec for front on next row and every other row once more—47 sts for front and 50 sts for back. Work even until neck opening measures 4½"/11.5cm. Tie yarn marker at front neck edge to mark center front. Work even until neck opening measures 7"/18cm, end with a WS row. **Next row (RS)** K50; k into back and front of next st (inc), k to end. Rep inc every other row twice more—50 sts for front and back. **Next row (WS)** P all 100 sts joining front and back. Work even until piece measures 60"/153cm from beg. Bind off.

FINISHING
Do not apply steam to finished piece.

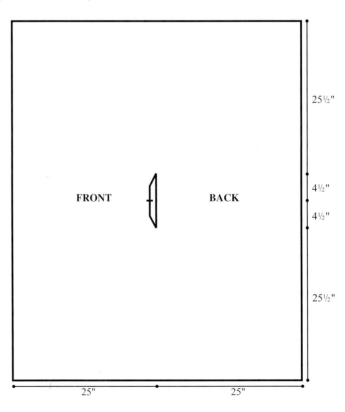

HOOD

Beg at center front neck marker, pick up and k 15 sts from right front neck, 31 sts from back neck and 15 sts from left front neck—61 sts. Do not join. Working back and forth in rows, work in St st until hood measures 10"/25.5cm, end with a WS row. Dec row K28, k2tog, pm, k1, pm, ssk, k28—59 sts. P 1 row. Cont to dec every other row by k2tog before first marker and ssk after 2nd marker 5 times more—49 sts. Bind off. Fold hood in half at center and sew top seam along bound-off edge. With crochet hook, work an edge of sc all around outer edge of poncho and around hood opening.

Floor-Length Vest

Have a little fashion fun with this maxi-length hooded vest. Designed by Rebecca Rosen, this cutting-edge cover-up is accented with oversized patch pockets and garter-stitch trim. Shown in size Medium. The Floor-Length Vest first appeared in the Fall '00 issue of *Vogue Knitting*.

VERY EASY VERY VOGUE

Floor-Length Vest

SIZES
To fit Small (Medium, Large, X-Large). Directions are for smallest size with larger sizes in parentheses. If there is only one figure, it applies to all sizes.

KNITTED MEASUREMENTS
● Bust 36½ (40½, 44½, 48½)"/92.5 (103, 113, 123)cm
● Length 56"/142cm

MATERIALS
● 1¾oz/50g balls (each approx 54yd/49m) of Classic Elite Yarns *Waterspun Weekend* (wool 5) in #35 green
● 14 (16, 17, 19) balls
● One zippper 18 (18, 19, 20)"/45.5 (45.5, 48.5, 51)cm long
● 2 toggles
● One pair size 15 (10mm) needles or SIZE TO OBTAIN GAUGE
● Stitch holders

GAUGE
8 sts = 4"/10cm and 13 rows = 5"/12.5cm over St st using size 15 (9mm) needles. FOR PERFECT FIT, TAKE TIME TO CHECK GAUGE.

BACK
Cast on 40 (44, 48, 52) sts. Work in garter st for 1½"/4cm, end with a WS row. Work in St st until piece measures 29½ (29½, 29, 28½)"/75 (75, 73.5, 72.5)cm from beg, end with a WS row. Dec row (RS) K2, SSK, k to last 4 sts, k2tog, k2—38 (42, 46, 50) sts. Work even until piece measures 37 (37, 36½, 36)"/94 (94, 92.5, 91.5)cm from beg, end with a WS row. Work dec row once more—36 (40, 44, 48) sts. Work even until piece measures 46½ (46½, 46, 45½)"/118 (118, 117, 115.5)cm from beg, end with a WS row.

Armhole shaping
Bind off 2 sts at beg of next 2 rows, 1 st at beg of next 2 rows. **Next row (RS)** Work dec row as for body. Work 1 row even. Rep last 2 rows 2 (2, 2, 3) times more—24 (28, 32, 34) sts. Work even until armhole measures 8 (8, 8½, 9)"/20.5 (20.5, 21.5, 23)cm, end with a WS row.

SHOULDER SHAPING
Bind off 2 (3, 4, 4) sts at beg of next 2 rows, 3 (4, 4, 5) sts at beg of next 2 rows. Place rem 14 (14, 16, 16) sts on holder for hood.

Pocket linings
(make 2)
Cast on 12 (14, 14, 14) sts and work in St st for 7"/18cm, place sts on holder.

LEFT FRONT
Cast on 22 (24, 26, 28) sts. Work in garter st for 1½"/4cm, end with a WS row. Work 3 sts at front edge (end of RS rows, beg of WS rows) in garter st and rem sts in St st until piece measures 29½ (29½, 29, 28½)"/75 (75, 73.5, 72.5)cm from beg, end with a WS row. Dec row (RS) K2, SSK, work to end—21 (23, 25, 27) sts. Work even until piece measures 34½ (34½, 34, 33½)"/87.5 (87.5, 86.5, 85)cm from beg, end with a WS row.

Insert pocket
Next row (RS) K4 (4, 6, 8), place next 12 (14, 14, 14) sts on holder and k12 (14, 14, 14) sts of one pocket lining, work to end. Work even until piece measures 37 (37, 36½, 36)"/94 (94, 92.5, 91.5)cm from beg, end with a WS row. Work dec row once more—20 (22, 24, 26) sts. Work even until piece measures 46½ (46½, 46, 45½)"/118 (118, 117, 115.5)cm from beg, end with a WS row.

Armhole shaping
Shape armhole at side edge only as for back—14 (16, 18, 19) sts. Work even until armhole measures 8 (8, 8½, 9)"/20.5 (20.5, 21.5, 23)cm, end with a WS row.

Neck and shoulder shaping
Next row (RS) Bind off 2 (3, 4, 4) sts at beg of row, work to end. **Next row** Place first 5 sts on holder, work to end. **Next row** Bind off 3 (4, 4, 5) sts at beg of row, work to end. Bind off rem 4 (4, 5, 5) sts.

RIGHT FRONT
Work as for left front, reversing all shaping.

FINISHING
Block all pieces to measurement. Sew shoulder seams.

Hood
With RS facing, including 5 sts from holder, pick up 12 sts evenly around

right neck, 14 (14, 16, 16) sts from back neck holder, 12 sts around left neck including 5 sts from holder – 38 (38, 40, 40) sts. Cont to work first and last 3 sts in garter st, work rem sts in St st for 3 rows. **Next row (RS)** Work 17 (17, 18, 18) sts, inc 1 st in next st, k2, inc 1 st in next st, work to end—40 (40, 42, 42) sts. Work 7 rows even. **Next row (RS)** Work 18 (18, 19, 19) sts, inc 1 st in next st, k2, inc 1 st in next st, work to end—42 (42, 44, 44) sts. Work even until hood mea-

sures 11 (11, 12, 12)"/28 (28, 30.5, 30.5)cm, end with a WS row. **Next row (RS)** Work 18 (18, 19, 19) sts, ssk, k2, k2tog, work to end—40 (40, 42, 42) sts. Work 1 row even. **Next row (RS)** Work 17 (17, 18, 18) sts, ssk, k2, k2tog, work to end—38 (38, 40, 40) sts. Work 1 row even. **Next row (RS)** Work 16 (16, 17, 17) sts, ssk, k2, k2tog, work to end—36 (36, 38, 38) sts. Work 1 row even. Dividing rem sts in half, knit sts tog.

Armhole trim

With RS facing, pick up 34 (34, 36, 38) sts evenly around armholes and work in garter st for 1"/2.5cm. Bind off all sts. Sew side seams.

Pocket trim

Pick up 12 (14, 14, 14) sts from pocket holders. Work in garter st for 1"/2.5cm. Bind off. Sew sides of garter trim to fronts. Sew pocket linings in place on WS.

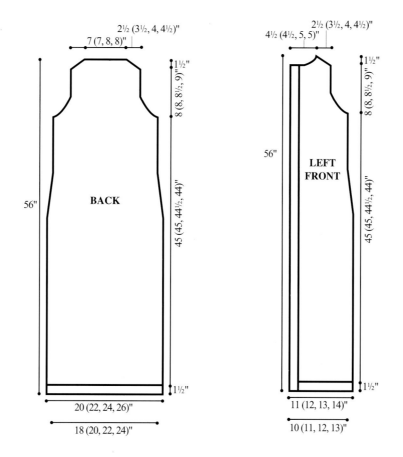

Free and easy. A twisted rib top compliments a simple garter-stitched cardigan in Viola Carol's classic twin set that works day to night for any occasion. Shown in size Small. The Textured Twin Set first appeared in the Spring/Summer '00 issue of *Vogue Knitting*.

Textured Twin Set

VERY EASY VERY VOGUE

SIZES
To fit X-Small (Small, Medium, Large). Twin set shown in size X-Small. Directions are for smallest size with larger sizes in parentheses. If there is only one figure, it applies to all sizes.

KNITTED MEASUREMENTS
Top
● Bust 26 (28, 30, 32)"/66 (71, 76, 81)cm
● Length 17 (17½, 18½, 19)"/43 (44.5, 47, 48)cm
Cardigan
● Bust 32 (34, 36, 38½)"/81 (86, 91.5, 98)cm
● Length 19 (19½, 20, 21)"/48 (49.5, 51, 53)cm
● Upper arm 12¼ (12¼, 13¼, 14½)"/31 (31, 33.5, 37)cm

MATERIALS
● 13 (14, 16, 17) 1¾oz/50g hanks (each approx 108yd/100m) of Tahki Yarns/Tahki•Stacy Charles, Inc. *Cotton Classic* (cotton 4) in #3066 pale grey (A)
● 8 (9, 9, 10) hanks in #3712 pale green (B)
● One pair size 8 (5mm) needles OR SIZE TO OBTAIN GAUGE
● Three ⅞"/22mm buttons

GAUGES
● 15 and 26 rows = 4"/10cm over garter st using double strand of yarn and size 8 (5mm) needles.

● 17 sts and 18 rows = 4"/10cm over twisted rib (slightly stretched) using double strand of yarn and size 8 (5mm) needles.
FOR PERFECT FIT, TAKE TIME TO CHECK GAUGES.

K1, P1 TWISTED RIB
(even number of sts)
Row 1 *K1 tbl, p1; rep from * to end.
Rep row 1 for k1, p1 twisted rib.

TOP

BACK
With double strand of B, cast on 50 (54, 58, 62) sts. Work in k1, p1 twisted rib for 2½"/6.5cm. Inc 1 st each side of next row then every 10th row twice more—56 (60, 64, 68) sts. Work even until piece measures 10 (10, 10½, 10½)"/25.5 (25.5, 26.5, 26.5)cm from beg.

Armhole shaping
Bind off 6 (6, 7, 7) sts at beg of next 2 rows—44 (48, 50, 54) sts. Work even until armhole measures 2 (2½, 3, 3½)"/5 (6.5, 7.5, 9)cm.

Neck shaping
Next row (RS) Work 15 sts in rib, join another double strand of yarn and bind off center 14 (18, 20, 24) sts, work to end. Work each 15-st strap separately until armhole measures 7 (7½, 8, 8½)"/18 (19, 20.5, 21.5)cm. Bind off in rib.

FRONT
Work as for back.

FINISHING
Block pieces lightly to measurements, being sure not to flatten ribs. Sew shoulder seams. Sew side seams.

CARDIGAN

BACK
With double strand of A, cast on 60 (64, 68, 72) sts. Work in garter st (k every row) until piece measures 11 (11½, 11½, 12)"/28 (29, 29, 30.5)cm from beg.

Armhole shaping
Bind off 5 (5, 6, 6) sts at beg of next 2 rows—50 (54, 56, 60) sts. Work even until armhole measures 8 (8, 8½, 9)"/20.5 (20.5, 21.5, 23)cm. Bind off.

LEFT FRONT
With double strand of A, cast on 36 (38, 40, 42) sts. Work in garter st until piece measures 11 (11½, 11½, 12)"/28 (29, 29, 30.5)cm from beg.

Armhole shaping
Bind off 5 (5, 6, 6) sts at beg of next RS row—31 (33, 34, 36) sts. Work even until armhole measures 5½ (5½, 6, 6½)"/14 (14, 15, 16.5)cm.

Neck shaping
Next row (WS) Bind off 10 (11, 11, 11) sts for neck, work to end. Cont to bind off 3 sts from neck edge every other row 1 (1, 2, 2) times, 2 sts 1 (1, 0, 0) time—16 (17, 17, 19) sts. When same length as back, bind off rem sts for shoulder.

RIGHT FRONT

Work to correspond to left front reversing neck shaping and working 3 buttonholes in center front edge as foll:
Buttonhole row (RS) K3, yo, k2tog, work to end. Work first buttonhole at 2½ (2½, 3, 3)"/6.5 (6.5, 7.5, 7.5)cm from lower edge, the other 2 at 4½ (4½, 4¾, 5)"/11.5 (11.5, 12, 12.5)cm intervals.

SLEEVES

With double strand of A, cast on 46 (46, 50, 54) sts. Work in garter st for 5"/12.5cm.

Cap shaping

Bind off 5 sts at beg of next 2 rows. Dec 1 st each side every 4th row 5 times, every other row 6 (6, 8, 10) times—14 sts. Bind off.

FINISHING

Block pieces to measurements. Sew shoulder seams.

Pockets

(make 2)
With double strand of B, cast on 19 sts. Work in garter st for 3"/7.5cm. Bind off. Sew pockets to fronts at 1½"/4cm from buttonhole and 1½"/4cm from lower edge.

Collar

With WS facing and double strand of B, beg at shaped neck edge, pick up and k 56 (58, 62, 62) sts evenly around neck edge. Work in garter st for 2½"/6.5cm, inc 1 st each side every 6th row twice—60 (62, 66, 66) sts. Bind off. Sew sleeves into armholes. Sew side and sleeve seams. Sew on buttons.

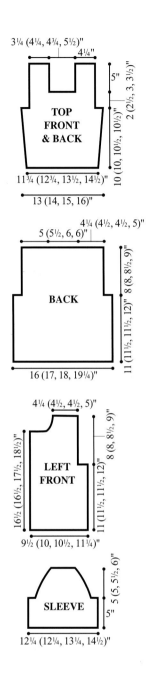

Double-Breasted Mohair Coat

Wrap yourself in style in a flowing floor-length coat. This Very Easy Very Vogue original, with set-in sleeves and notched collar, gets wonderful surface design from a knit-purl box stitch. Shown in size Medium. The Double-Breasted Mohair Coat first appeared in the Fall '96 issue of *Vogue Knitting*.

VERY EASY VERY VOGUE

Double-Breasted Mohair Coat

SIZES
To Small (Medium, Large). Directions are for smallest size with larger sizes in parentheses. If there is only one figure, it applies to all sizes.

KNITTED MEASUREMENTS
● Bust (with garment closed) 42 (45, 49)"/106.5 (114.5, 124.5)cm.
● Length 50 (52½, 55)"/ 127 (132, 139.5)cm.
● Sleeve width at upper arm 17 (17, 18½)"/ 43 (43, 47)cm

MATERIALS
Original Yarn
● 10 (11, 12) 1½oz/43g balls (each approx 93yd/85m) each of Berroco, Inc. *Mohair Classic* (mohair/wool/nylon 4 ll) in #1137 turquoise and #1138 blue.
● 9 (10, 11) 1¾oz/50g balls (each approx 99yd/90m) of Lang/Berroco *Rivoli* (mohair/ nylon/acrylic 4) in # 8917 blue/green
Substitute Yarn
● 11 (12, 13) 1¾oz/50g balls (each approx 90yd/83m) of Berroco, Inc. *Furz* (nylon/wool/acrylic 4) in #3835 teal (B)
● 10 (11, 12) 1½oz/43g balls (each approx 93yd/85m) of Mohair Classic (mohair/wool/nylon 4) in #6404 (A)

● One pair size 13 (9mm) needles OR SIZE TO OBTAIN GAUGE.
● Stitch holders.
● Eight ¾"/20mm buttons.

Note
The original yarn used for this sweater is no longer available. A comparable substitute has been made, which is available at the time of printing. Check gauge of substitute yarns very carefully before beginning.

GAUGE
16 sts to 7"/18cm and 12 rows to 4"/10cm over pat st with three strands of yarn held together.
FOR PERFECT FIT, TAKE TIME TO CHECK GAUGE.

Note
Coat is worked with 2 strands of A and 1 strand of B held together throughout.

STITCH GLOSSARY

KNIT/PURL BOX ST
Rows 1 & 3 (RS) K4, * p4, k4* rep between *'s.
Rows 2 & 4 P4, * k4, p4*; rep between *'s.
Rows 5 & 7 (RS) P4, * k4, p4*: rep between *'s.
Rows 6 & 8 K4, * p4, k4*; rep between *'s.

BACK
With 3 strands of yarn held together, cast on 48 (52, 56) sts.
Rows 1 & 3 (RS) K2 (4, 2), *p4, k4*; rep between *'s to last 2 (4, 2) sts, end k2 (4, 2).
Rows 2 & 4 (WS) P2 (4, 2), *k4, p4*; rep between *'s to last 2 (4, 2) sts, end p2 (4, 2).
Rows 5 & 7 P2, (4, 2), * k4, p4*; rep between *'s to last 2 (4, 2) sts, end p2,(4, 2).
Rows 6 & 8 K2 (4, 2) *p4, k4*; rep from * to last 2 (4, 2) sts, end k2 (4, 2). Repeat these 8 rows until piece measures 40 (42, 44)"/ 101.5 (106.5, 111.5)cm from beg, or desired length, end with (WS) row 4 or 8 of pat st WS row.

Armhole shaping
Working in established pat, bind off 2 sts beg of next 4 rows. Dec 1 st each side every other row 2 (2, 3) times, every 4th row 2 (2, 1) times—32 (36, 40) sts. Work even until armhole measures 9 (9½,10)" / 23 (24.5, 25.5) cm.

Shoulder shaping
Next row (RS) Bind off 6 (6, 8) sts beg of next 2 (4, 2) rows, then 4 (0, 0) sts at beg 2 rows. Place remaining 12 sts on holder for back of neck.

LEFT FRONT
Cast on 30 (32, 34) sts. Beg pat st with row 1, work in pat until front measures same as back to armhole, end with WS row.

Armhole shaping
Shape armhole at side edge (beg of RS row) as for back—22 (24, 26) sts. Work even until armhole measures 6 (6½, 7)"/15 (16.5, 17.5) cm end with RS row

Neck shaping

Next row (WS) Bind off 10 sts (neck edge), cont in pat, work to end. Dec 1 st from neck edge every other row 2 times—10 (12, 14) sts. AT SAME TIME, when same length as back to shoulder, shape shoulder at side edge as for back. Mark placement of four buttons place first marker 4 sts from edge and on 6th block down from neck, then every 4th block down, 3 times.

RIGHT FRONT

Work to correspond to left front, reversing shaping and work each buttonhole opposite markers on RS row as foll: (on "knit" blocks) k2, k2tog, YO, work to end; OR (on "purl" blocks) p2, p2tog, YO, work to end.

SLEEVES

Cast on 28 sts. Beg pat st (RS) with row 1. work in pat. AT SAME TIME, inc 1 st each side on 5th row once, and every 8th row 5 (5, 6) times—40 (40, 42) sts. Work even until sleeve measures 17 (17½, 18)"/ 43.5 (44.5, 46)cm, from beg or desired length, end WS row.

Cap shaping

Bind off 2 sts at beg of next 14 rows, 3 sts at beg of next 2 rows. Bind off rem 6 (6, 8) sts.

FINISHING

Lightly block pieces to measurements. Sew shoulder seams.

Collar

With RS facing and beg at 4"/10 cm in from right front neck edge (end of bind offs) pick up 12 sts along right front neck edge 12 sts from holder and 12 sts along left front neck edge ending with 4"/10cm end from left front neck edge— 36 sts. **Row 1 (RS)** Work in pat st. **Rows 2—4** Cont in pat. **Row 5 (RS)** Inc 1 st each side on next and every other row, until 48 sts. Bind off loosely. Sew side and sleeve seams, set-in sleeves. Sew on buttons.

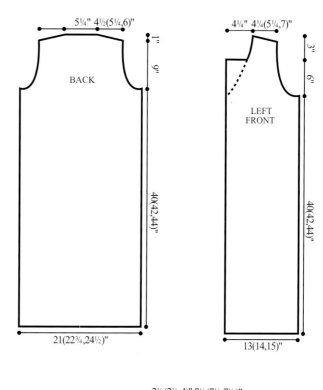

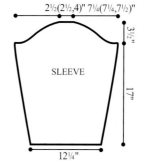

A gorgeous yarn can transform a simple garment into a work of wearable art. Peggy MacKenzie's chunky hooded poncho knits up quick in a plush thick-and-thin yarn. One size fits all. The Easy Hooded Poncho first appeared in the Fall '00 issue of *Vogue Knitting*.

Easy Hooded Poncho

VERY EASY VERY VOGUE

SIZES
One size fits all.

KNITTED MEASUREMENTS
● Lower edge 72"/183cm
● Length 26"/66cm at point

MATERIALS
● 8 3½oz/100g skeins (each approx 54yd/50m) of Colinette/Unique Kolours *Point 5* (wool 6) in #89 dk umber
● Size 19 (16mm) circular needle, 29"/74cm long OR SIZE TO OBTAIN GAUGE
● Size 11 (8mm) circular needle, 18"/45cm long
● Size M (9mm) crochet hook
● Stitch markers

GAUGE
8 sts = 5"/20.5cm and 10 rows = 4"/10cm over St st using larger circular needle.
FOR PERFECT FIT, TAKE TIME TO CHECK GAUGE.

Note
To ensure an even distribution of color, work with 2 balls of yarn at once, changing balls every other row and carrying yarn up sides without cutting.

BACK
Beg at lower edge with larger circular needle, loosely cast on 74 sts. Beg with a WS row, k37, pm for center of row, k37. **Row 1 (RS)** K35, k2tog, sl marker, SKP, k35. **Row 2** and all even rows Purl. **Row 3** K to 2 sts before marker, k2tog; sl marker, SKP, k to end. **Row 5** K7, p14, k12, k2tog; SKP, k4, p11, k18. **Row 7** K4, p5, k14, p5, k4, k2tog; SKP, k14, p12, k6. **Row 9** K31, k2tog; SKP, k31. **Row 11** K14, p8, k8, k2tog; SKP, k9, p8, k13. **Row 13** K23, p6, k2tog; SKP, k2, p5, k22. **Row 15** K5, p12, k11, k2tog; SKP, k12, p12, k4. **Row 17** K27, k2tog; SKP, k27. **Row 19** K16, p7, k3, k2tog; SKP, k5, p10, k11. **Row 21** K5, p14, k6, k2tog; SKP, k15, p4, k6. **Row 23** K24, k2tog, SKP, k24. **Row 25** K14, p7, k2, k2tog; SKP, k5, p9, k9. **Row 27** K7, p4, k11, k2tog, SKP, k22. **Row 29** K3, p6, k12, k2tog; SKP, k11, p6, k4. **Row 31** K12, p5, k3, k2tog; SKP, k2, p4, k14. **Row 33** K19, k2tog; SKP, k19. **Row 35** K11, p4, k3, k2tog; SKP, k3, p6, k9. **Row 37** K2tog, k15, M1, k2tog; SKP, M1, k15, k2tog. **Row 39** K2tog, k14, M1, k2tog; SKP, M1, k14, k2tog. **Row 41** K2tog, p8, k5, M1, k2tog; SKP, M1, k5, p6, k2, k2tog. **Row 43** K2tog, k12, M1, k2tog, SKP, M1, k12, k2tog. **Row 45** K2tog, k5, p6, M1, k2tog, SKP, M1, k11, k2tog. **Row 47** K2tog, k10, M1, k2tog; SKP, M1, k2, p6, k2, k2tog—26 sts. Place sts on a holder.

FRONT
Work as for back.

Join front and back
With smaller circular needle, k26 sts of front, k26 sts of back—52 sts. Join, pm to mark beg of rnd and work in rnds of k1, p1 rib for 5 rnds. Next rnd Rib 9 sts, bind off 8 sts (for center front neck), rib to end. Turn work to work back and forth in rows.

HOOD
Change to larger circular needle. **Next row (WS)** Purl, dec 4 sts evenly spaced—40 sts. Work even in St st for 21 rows.

Top shaping
Next row (WS) P20 and leave these st to be worked later, bind off 6 sts, p to end. **Next row (RS)** K14, turn. **Next row** Bind off 7 sts, p to end. **Next row** K7. **Next row** Bind off 7 sts. Rejoin yarn from RS to work rem 20 sts and bind off 6 sts, work to end. **Next row** P14. **Next row** Bind off 7 sts, work to end. **Next row** P7. Bind off 7 sts.

FINISHING
Block to measurements. Sew hood seam. Sew side seams. With crochet hook, work an edge of sc along hood opening. Ch 1, do not turn. Working backwards (from left to right), work 1 backwards sc in each sc.

Rosemary Drysdale's buttonless cardigan with a reverse pocket is the crème de la crème of classic elegance. Stitched in easy stockinette, it knits quickly in a lofty wool yarn. Shown in size Small. The Drop-Shoulder Cardigan first appeared in the Winter '00/'01 issue of *Vogue Knitting*.

Drop-Shoulder Cardigan

VERY EASY VERY VOGUE

SIZES
To fit Small (Medium, Large, X-Large, XX-Large). Directions are for smallest size with larger sizes in parentheses. If there is only one figure, it applies to all sizes.

KNITTED MEASUREMENTS
● Bust (closed) 40 (44, 48, 52, 56)"/101.5 (111.5, 122, 132, 142)cm
● Length 20 (20½, 21½, 22, 23)"/50.5 (52, 54.5, 56, 58.5)cm
● Upper arm 15 (16, 17, 18, 20)"/38 (41, 43, 46, 51)cm

MATERIALS
● 11 (12, 13, 15, 16) 3½oz/100g balls (each approx 55yd/50m) of Filatura Di Crosa/Tahki•Stacy Charles, Inc. *Air Wool* (wool/microacrylic 5) in #1 ecru
● One pair size 13 (9mm) needles OR SIZE TO OBTAIN GAUGE

GAUGE
9 sts and 14 rows = 4"/10cm over St st using size 13 (9mm) needles.
FOR PERFECT FIT, TAKE TIME TO CHECK GAUGE.

BACK
Cast on 46 (50, 55, 59, 64) sts. Work in St st for 12½ (12½, 13, 13, 13)"/31.5 (31.5, 33, 33, 33)cm, end with a WS row.

Armhole shaping
Next row (RS) K2, SKP, work to end.

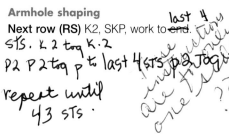

Work one row even. Rep last 2 rows 1 (2, 2, 2, 2) times more. **Next row (RS)** K2, SKP, work to end. **Next row** Work, p to last 4 sts, p2tog tbl, p2. Rep last 2 rows until there are 38 (40, 43, 47, 50) sts. Work even until armhole measures 7½ (8, 8½, 9, 10)"/19 (20.5, 21.5, 23, 25.5)cm. Bind off all sts.

LEFT FRONT
Cast on 23 (25, 27, 30, 32) sts. Work St st, working 2 sts in garter st at front edge (end of RS rows, beg of WS rows) for 7"/17.5cm. Place a marker each end of row for pocket. Work even until piece measures 12½ (12½, 13, 13, 13)"/31.5 (31.5, 33, 33, 33)cm above markers, end with a WS row.

Armhole shaping
Next row (RS) K2, SKP, work to end. Work 1 row even. Rep last 2 rows 1 (2, 2, 2, 2) times more. **Next row (RS)** K2, SKP, work to end. **Next row** Work to last 4 sts, p2tog tbl, p2. Rep last 2 rows until there are 19 (20, 21, 24, 25) sts. Work even until armhole measures 5½ (6, 6½, 7, 8)"/14 (15.5, 16.5, 18, 20.5)cm, end with a RS row.

Neck shaping
Next row (WS) Bind off 5 (5, 5, 6, 6) sts (neck edge), work to end. Cont to dec 1 st at neck edge on next row, then every row twice more. Work even until same length as back. Bind off rem 11 (12, 13, 15, 16) sts for shoulder.

RIGHT FRONT
Work to correspond to left front, reversing shaping and placement of garter st edge.

SLEEVES
Cast on 20 (21, 21, 21, 22) sts. Work St st, inc 1 st each side every 8th (6th, 6th, 6th, 4th) row 5 (2, 5, 9, 4) times, every 10th (8th, 8th, 8th, 6th) row 2 (6, 4, 1, 8) times—34 (37, 39, 41, 46) sts. Work even until piece measures 18½ (18½, 19, 19, 19½)"/(47, 47, 48.5, 48.5, 49.5)cm from beg.

Cap shaping
Next row (RS) K2, SKP, k to last 4 sts k2tog, k2. P 1 row. Rep last 2 rows 1 (2, 2, 2, 2) times more. **Next row (RS)** K2, SKP, k to last 4 sts k2tog, k2. **Next row** P2, p2tog, p to last 4 sts, p2tog tbl, p2. Rep last 2 rows until there are 26 (27, 27, 29, 32) sts. Bind off.

FINISHING
Block pieces to measurements. Sew shoulder seams.

Neckband
With RS facing, pick up and k 42 (42, 44, 44, 46) sts evenly around neck edge. Beg with a k row, work in rev St st for 12 rows. Bind off loosely. Fold neckband in half to WS and sew in place (p side will show). Fold up pockets to markers (p side will show) and sew to front edge. Set in sleeves. Sew side and sleeve seams, sewing through all thicknesses at sides.

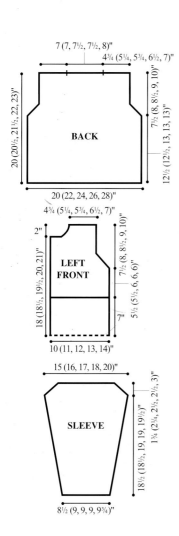

7 (7, 7½, 7½, 8)"

4¾ (5¼, 5¾, 6½, 7)"

20 (20½, 21½, 22, 23)"

BACK

7½ (8, 8½, 9, 10)"

12½ (12½, 13, 13, 13)"

20 (22, 24, 26, 28)"

4¾ (5¼, 5¾, 6½, 7)"

2"

18 (18½, 19½, 20, 21)"

LEFT FRONT

7½ (8, 8½, 9, 10)"

7½ (8, 6, 6, 6)"

5½ (5½, 6, 6, 6)"

7"

10 (11, 12, 13, 14)"

15 (16, 17, 18, 20)"

SLEEVE

18½ (18½, 19, 19, 19½)"

1¾ (2¼, 2¼, 2½, 3)"

8½ (9, 9, 9, 9¾)"

Joan Vass puts a sophisticated spin on the timeless poncho with a face-framing turtleneck and smooth shoulder shaping. It's worked from the top down so length can be customized to the wearer. Two strands of yarn held together make for speedy stitching. Shown in size Medium. The Fringed Turtleneck Poncho first appeared in the Winter'99/'00 issue of *Vogue Knitting*.

Fringed Turtleneck Poncho

VERY EASY VERY VOGUE

SIZES
To fit Small (Medium, Large). Directions are for smallest size with larger sizes in parentheses. If there is only one figure, it applies to all sizes.

KNITTED MEASUREMENTS
● Width at widest point 46"/117cm
● Length from center back neck (without fringe) 31"/78.5cm

MATERIALS
● 10 3½oz/100g balls (each approx 183yd/167m) of Tahki Yarns/Tahki•Stacy Charles, Inc. *Donegal Tweed* (wool 5) in #801 green
● Two size 13 circular needles, 24"/60cm and 40"/100cm long
● Stitch markers

GAUGE
10 sts and 15 rows = 4"/10cm over St st using size 13 needles and 2 strands of yarn held tog.
FOR PERFECT FIT, TAKE TIME TO CHECK GAUGE.

Notes
1 Poncho is worked from the neck down.
2 Work with two strands of yarn held tog throughout.

PONCHO
With 2 strands of yarn held tog, cast on 56 sts. Join, taking care not to twist sts on needle. Place marker for end of rnd and sl marker every rnd. Work in k2, p2 rib for 9"/23cm.

Note
When placing markers on the foll rnd, use different markers than the end of rnd marker for easier knitting. Slip all markers on every rnd.

Next rnd K1, pm (center back), k14, pm (center shoulder), k14, pm (center front), k14, pm (center shoulder), k13.
Next rnd K1, yo, [k13, yo, k1, yo] 3 times, k13, yo. K 1 rnd.
Next rnd K1, yo, k1 [k14, yo, k1, yo, k1] 3 times, k14, yo. K 1 rnd.
Next rnd K1, yo, k2, [k15, yo, k1, yo, k2] 3 times, k15, yo. K 1 rnd.
Rep last 2 rnds 5 times more, working one more k st before and after every yo, k1, yo, every other rnd.
Remove 2nd and 4th markers (at shoulders). Cont working yo, k1, yo every other rnd at center back and front only, working rem sts as knit, for 74 rows (or 37 eyelets after shoulder eyelets). Piece should measure approx 22"/56cm from last shoulder eyelets. Bind off all sts.

FRINGE
Using 3 strands for each fringe, attach fringe (4"/10cm finished length) along lower edge of poncho (see photo).

A combination of three different hand-dyed yarns creates the subtle striping and sumptuous texture on Mari Lynn Patrick's standout coat. Cuffs and collars are worked in a plush wool/nylon yarn for a stylish contrast. Shown in size Medium. The Textured Coat first appeared in the Fall '00 issue of *Vogue Knitting*.

Textured Coat

VERY EASY VERY VOGUE

SIZES
To fit Small (Medium, Large, X-Large). Directions are for smallest size with changes for larger sizes in parentheses. If there is only one figure is applies to all sizes.

KNITTED MEASUREMENTS
● Lower edge 54 (56, 58, 60)"/137 (142, 147, 152)cm
● Bust 40 (42, 44, 46)"/102 (107, 112, 117)cm
● Length 36 (36½, 36½, 36½)"/91.5 (92.5, 92.5, 92.5)cm
● Upper arm 17 (18, 19, 19¾)"/43 (45.5, 48, 50)cm

MATERIALS
● 2 1¾oz/50g balls (each approx 48yd/44m) of kIC2 LLC *Flureece* (wool/nylon 5) in #146 ivory (A)
● 8 (8, 9, 9) 1¾oz/50g balls (each approx 112yd/102m) of *Mousse* (mohair/wool/nylon 4) in #6111 cream (B)
● 8 (8, 9, 9) 1¾oz/50g balls (each approx 105yd/96m) of *Bon Bon* (mohair/wool/nylon 4) in #5111 cream (C)
● 3 (3, 3, 4) 3½oz/100g balls (each approx 218yd/200m) of *Parfait Solids* in #1101 ecru (D-4)
● 2 (2, 2, 3) balls in #2822 beige (D-1)
● 1 ball each in #2811 taupe (D-2) and #1798 purple (D-3)
● One pair each sizes 10 and 13 (6 and 9mm) needles OR SIZE TO OBTAIN GAUGE
● Stitch holders
● Three 1"/25mm triangular buttons

GAUGE
● 14 sts and 18 rows = 6"/15cm over St st using size larger needles and 1 strand each B, C and D-1, 2, 3 or 4.
● 10 sts and 16 rows = 4"/10cm over reverse St st using smaller needles. FOR PERFECT FIT, TAKE TIME TO CHECK GAUGE.

STRIPE PATTERN
Stripe pat is worked in St st using larger needles and 1 strand each B, C and D-1, 2, 3 or 4 as foll: *Work 14 rows with D-1, 10 rows with D-4, 2 rows with D-3, 10 rows with D-4, 2 rows with D-2, 10 rows with D-4, 8 rows with D-1, 4 rows with D-3; rep from * (60 rows) for stripe pat.

BACK
With larger needles and 1 strand each B, C and D-1 held tog, cast on 63 (65, 67, 70). Work in reverse St st for 5 rows. Then cont in St st and stripe pat and work even for 18 rows more. Dec 1 st each side of next row then every 8th row 4 times more, every 6th row 3 times—47 (49, 51, 54) sts. Work even until piece measures 26 (26, 25½, 25)"/66 (66, 65, 63.5)cm from beg.

Armhole shaping
Bind off 2 sts at beg of next 2 rows. Dec 1 st each side of next row then every other row 3 times more—35 (37, 39, 42) sts. Work even until armhole measures 9 (9½, 10, 10½)"/23 (24, 25.5, 26.5)cm.

Neck and shoulder shaping
Bind off 5 sts at beg of next 2 rows, 5 (5, 6) sts at beg of next 2 rows, AT SAME TIME, bind off center 11 (13, 15, 16) sts for neck and working both sides at once, bind off 2 sts from each neck edge once.

LEFT FRONT
With larger needles and 1 strand each B, C and D-1 held tog, cast on 36 (37, 38, 40) sts. Work in reverse St st for 5 rows.

Beg St st and stripe pat.
Next row (WS) P4, k1 (front band), p to end. **Next row** K to last 5 sts, p5. Rep last 2 rows for 5-st front band until there are 18 rows in St st. Dec 1 st at armhole edge on next row and rep every 8th row 4 times more, every 6th row 3 times—28 (29, 30, 32) sts. Work even until piece measures same as back to armhole.

Armhole shaping
Next row (RS) Bind off 2 sts, work to end. Cont to shape armhole dec 1 st at armhole edge every other row 4 times—22 (23, 24, 26) sts. Work even until armhole measures 4½ (5, 5½, 6)"/11.5 (12.5, 14, 15.5)cm.

Neck shaping
Next row (WS) Sl 5 sts to a holder, bind off next 2 (2, 3, 3) sts, work to end. Cont to dec 1 st at neck edge every other row 6 (6, 6, 7) times. When same length as back, bind off 5 sts from shoulder edge once and 4 (5, 5, 6) sts once.

RIGHT FRONT
Work to correspond to left front reversing shaping and 5-st front band and working 3 yo, k2tog buttonholes in band, the first one at 21"/53cm from beg

and the others at 5"/12.5cm intervals.

SLEEVES

With smaller needles and A, cast on 24 (26, 26, 28) sts very loosely. Beg with a WS (knit) row, work in reverse St st for 3"/7.5cm. Change to larger needles and cont in St st and stripe pat inc 1 st each side every 6th row 4 (4, 3, 3) times every 4th row 4 (4, 6, 6) times—40 (42, 44, 46) sts. Work even until piece measures 18"/45.5cm from beg.

Cap shaping

Bind off 2 sts at beg of next 4 rows, dec 1 st each side of next row then every other row 7 (8, 8, 9) times more. Bind off 3 sts at beg of next 2 rows. Bind off.

FINISHING

Block piece to measurements. Sew shoulder seams. Sew sleeves into armholes. Sew side and sleeve seams.

COLLAR

With smaller needles and A, pick up and k 44 (44, 48, 50) sts evenly around neck edge including sts from holders. Cont the first and last 5 sts in front band pat as before, work rem sts in reverse St st for 5"/12.5cm. Bind off very loosely. Sew on buttons.

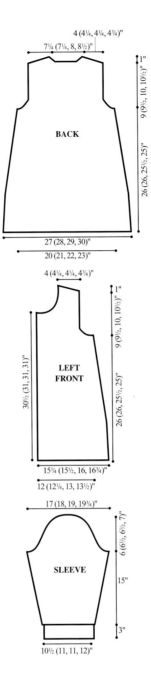

BACK

4 (4¼, 4¼, 4¾)"

7¼ (7¼, 8, 8½)"

1"

9 (9½, 10, 10½)"

26 (26, 25½, 25)"

27 (28, 29, 30)"

20 (21, 22, 23)"

LEFT FRONT

4 (4¼, 4¼, 4¾)"

1"

9 (9½, 10, 10½)"

30½ (31, 31, 31)"

26 (26, 25½, 25)"

15¼ (15½, 16, 16¾)"

12 (12¼, 13, 13½)"

SLEEVE

17 (18, 19, 19¾)"

6 (6½, 6½, 7)"

15"

3"

10½ (11, 11, 12)"

Easy Elegance

Simplicity at its best—
embrace the
softer side of style
in fabulous looks
that take you from
day to night.

Linda Cyr uses fluted texture to turn a simple wrap into a stunning fashion statement. The striking geometric pattern, created by easy combinations of knit and purl stitches, is trimmed with a scattering of bobbles. One size fits all. The Bobble-Trimmed Shawl first appeared in the Fall '97 issue of *Vogue Knitting*.

Bobble-Trimmed Shawl

VERY EASY VERY VOGUE

SIZES
One size fits all.

KNITTED MEASUREMENTS
- 18" x 72"/46cm x 183cm

MATERIALS
- 10 1¾oz/50g skeins (each approx 107yd/ 98m) Lion Brand *AL•PA•KA* (acrylic/alpaca/ wool 4) in #124 camel (MC)
- 1 skein in #153 black (CC)
- Size 7 (4.5mm) circular needle 24"/61cm long OR SIZE NEEDED TO OBTAIN GAUGE
- Size G (4.5mm) crochet hook

GAUGE
18 sts and 24 rows to 4"/10cm in St st (check gauge in St st as pat st falls into pleats).
FOR PERFECT FIT, TAKE TIME TO CHECK GAUGE.

STITCH GLOSSARY
Bobble
K1, p1, k1, p1, k1 in one st, turn. Work 7 rows Garter st over 5 sts. **Next row** Sl 3 sts knitwise, k3tog tbl, place st on LH needle, k3tog, place st on LH needle. Insert RH needle into base of bobble (original first st), psso st on LH needle. Fluted Rib (multiple of 8 sts plus 1)
Rows 1-3 P1, *k1, p1; rep from *. **Row 4** K2, *p5, k3; rep from *, end p5, k2. **Row 5** P3, *k3, p5; rep from *, end k3, p3. **Row 6-8** K4, *p1, k7; rep from *, end p1, k4. **Row 9** Rep row 5. **Row 10** rep row 4. Rep rows 1-10 for pat.

Note
Always start a new skein of yarn at beg of row.

WRAP
With CC, cast on 97 sts. **Row 1** *Make bobble (MB), k7; rep from *, end MB. **Rows 2 and 3** Knit, **Row 4** Change to MC, *k1, p1; rep from *, end k1. Beg fluted rib pat, cont until piece measures 70"/178cm from beg, end with a WS row. **Next row** Change to CC (do not cut MC), *k1, p1; rep from *, end k1. Knit the next 2 rows. **Next row** *MB, k1, psso (counts as first bind off), bind off 7 more sts; rep from *, end MB. Cut CC yarn, pull through.

FINISHING
Pick up MC, with crochet hook, work 1 row of rev sc along side edge, fasten off. Rep for other side. Block lightly.

With minimal shaping, Rebecca Rosen's ultra-easy zippered vest works for day or evening. It's a super-quick knit in a distinctive polar plush yarn. Shown in size Small. The Zip-Front Vest first appeared in the Winter '00/'01 issue of *Vogue Knitting*.

Zip-Front Vest

VERY EASY VERY VOGUE

SIZES
To fit Small (Medium, Large, X-Large). Directions are for smallest size with larger sizes in parentheses. If there is only one figure, it applies to all sizes.

KNITTED MEASUREMENTS
● Bust (zippered) 36 (40½, 43½, 48)"/91.5 (103, 110.5, 122)cm
● Length 20"/51cm

MATERIALS
● 5 (6, 7, 7) 1¾oz/50g balls (each approx 48yds/45m) of Mondial/Skacel Collection *Fur* (wool/acrylic/polyester 6) in #86 ecru
● One pair size 10½ (6.5mm) needles OR SIZE TO OBTAIN GAUGE
● 18"/46cm long zipper

GAUGE
12 sts and 23 rows = 5"/12.5cm over rev St st.
FOR PERFECT FIT, TAKE TIME TO CHECK GAUGE.

BACK
Cast on 43 (48, 53, 58) sts. Work in rev St st for 11½ (11, 10½, 10)"/29.5 (28, 27, 25.5)cm, end with a WS row.

Armhole shaping
Bind off 2 sts at beg of next 2 rows. Dec 1 st each side on next row, then every other row 2 (2, 2, 3) times more—33 (38, 43, 46) sts. Work even until armhole measures 7½ (8, 8½, 9)"/19 (20.5, 21.5, 23)cm, end with a WS row.

Neck and shoulder shaping
Bind off 4 (5, 6, 6) sts at beg of next 2 rows, 4 (5, 6, 7) sts at beg of next 2 rows, AT SAME TIME, bind off center 15 (16, 17, 18) sts for neck, and working both sides at once, dec 1 st at each neck edge every other row once.

LEFT FRONT
Cast on 22 (24, 25, 29) sts. Work in rev St st for 11½ (11, 10½, 10)"/29.5 (28, 27, 25.5)cm, end with a WS row.

Armhole shaping
Next row (RS) Bind off 2 sts (armhole edge), work to end. Work 1 row even. Dec 1 st at beg of next row, then every other row 2 (2, 2, 3) times more—17 (19, 20, 23) sts. Work even until armhole measures 6½ (7, 7½, 8)"/16.5 (18, 19, 20.5)cm, end with a RS row.

Neck and shoulder shaping
Next row (WS) Bind off 5 (5, 4, 5) sts at beg of row (neck edge), and cont to bind off and dec from neck edge 2 (2, 2, 3) sts once, 1 st twice, AT SAME TIME, when piece measures same length as back to shoulder, shape shoulder as for back.

RIGHT FRONT
Work as for left front, reversing all shaping.

FINISHING
Block pieces to measurement. Sew shoulder seams. Sew side seams. Set in zipper.

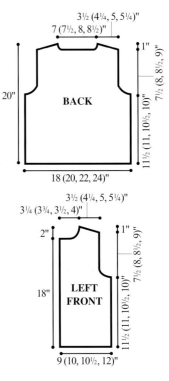

A bouquet of ruffled satin ribbon swirls across the yoke of this exquisite evening top by Susan McCaffrey. Worked in simple stockinette with raglan sleeves and ribbed edging, it's a timeless classic. Shown in size 34. The Ribbon-Trimmed Pullover first appeared in the Holiday '88 issue of *Vogue Knitting*.

Ribbon-Trimmed Pullover

VERY EASY VERY VOGUE

SIZES

To fit 30 (32, 34, 36, 38)"/76 (81, 86, 91, 96)cm bust. Directions are for smallest size with larger sizes in parentheses. If there is only one figure it applies to all sizes.

KNITTED MEASUREMENTS

- Bust 32 (34, 36, 38, 40)"/80 (84, 90, 94, 100)cm.
- Length 18¼ (19, 19½, 20¼, 21¼)"/45.5 (48, 49, 51, 53)cm.
- Sleeve width at upper arm 14½ (15, 15¾, 16, 16½)"/36 (37, 39, 40, 41)cm.

MATERIALS

Original Yarn

- 8 (8, 9, 9, 10) 1¾oz/50g balls (each approx 137yd/125m) of Aarlan *Royal* (wool/acrylic/mohair 3) in #4243 olive
- 1 spool (each approx 100yd/90m) of Studio 2 Ltd. *½ Ribbon* (rayon 5) in #29 olive or seam binding
- One pair each sizes 3 and 5 (3.25 and 3.75mm) needles OR SIZE TO OBTAIN GAUGE
- Size 3 (3.25mm) circular needle 16"/40cm

Substitute Yarn

- 5 (5, 6, 6, 7) 3½oz/100g balls (each approx 223yd/205m) of Patons® *Classic Merino Wool* (wool 3) in #205
- 1 spool (each approx 100yd/91m) of *Mokuba* in matching color or seam binding
- One pair each sizes 4 and 6 (3.5 and 4mm) needles OR SIZE TO OBTAIN GAUGE
- Size 4 (3.5mm) circular needle 16/ 40cm

Note

The original yarn used for this sweater is no longer available. A comparable substitute has been made, which is available at the time of printing. Check gauge of substitute yarns very carefully before beginning.

GAUGE

20 sts and 30 rows to 4"/10cm over St st using size 5 (3.75mm) needles. FOR PERFECT FIT, TAKE TIME TO CHECK GAUGE.

BACK

With smaller needles, cast on 96 (100, 106, 110, 116) sts. **Rib row 1** *K1, p1; rep from * to end. Rep last row for rib for 3"/7.5cm, dec 28 sts evenly across last row—68 (72, 78, 82, 88) sts. Change to larger needles. Work in St st (k on RS, p on WS), inc 1 st each side every 6th row 3 (1, 1, 0, 0) times, every 8th row 3 (5, 5, 5, 3) times, every 10th row 0 (0, 0, 1, 3) times—80 (84, 90, 94, 100) sts. Work even until piece measures 9½ (10, 10, 10½, 11)"/24 (25.5, 25.5, 26,5, 27.5)cm from beg, end with a WS row.

Raglan shaping

Bind off 4 (4, 5, 5, 5) sts at beg of next 2 rows. Dec 1 st each side of next row, then alternately every 4th and 2nd row (therefore 4 sts dec every 6 rows), until there are 40 (42, 44, 46, 50) sts. Bind off.

FRONT

Work as for back, including armhole shaping, until there are 46 (48, 50, 52, 56) sts, end with a WS row.

Neck shaping

Cont raglan dec, bind off center 34 (36, 38, 40, 44) sts on next row, then bind off from each neck edge 3 sts once. Bind off rem 2 sts each side.

RIGHT SLEEVE

With smaller needles, cast on 46 (46, 48, 50, 50) sts. Work in rib as for back for 2"/5cm. Change to larger needles and St st, inc 1 st every 6th row 13 (14, 15, 15, 16) times—72 (74, 78, 80, 82) sts. Work even until piece measures 15 (15½, 16, 16, 16½)"/37.5 (38.5, 39.5, 39.5, 41.5)cm from beg.

Raglan shaping

Bind off 4 (4, 5, 5, 5) sts at beg of next 2 rows. Dec 1 st each side of next row, then alternately every 4th and 2nd row until there are 36 sts, end with a WS row. **Next row (RS)** Bind off 11 sts (front edge), work to end, cont raglan dec. Cont to bind off from front edge 11 sts twice more, working raglan dec at back edge. Fasten off last st.

LEFT SLEEVE

Work as for right sleeve, reversing raglan shaping at top of sleeve.

FINISHING

Block pieces. Sew back edge (long side) of raglan sleeve to back armhole and front edge (short side) of sleeve to front armhole. Sew side and sleeve seams.

Neckband

With RS facing and circular needle, pick up and k120 (126, 134, 138, 148) sts. Join. Work in k1, p1 rib for 1"/2.5cm. Bind off in rib.

Ribbon swirls

With contrasting yarn or thread, baste a circular yoke line, beg 6½"/16.5cm down from rib (guideline for working swirls). Using a matching thread, gather ribbon and sew to sweater in swirl pattern as desired, taking care not to pull tightly.

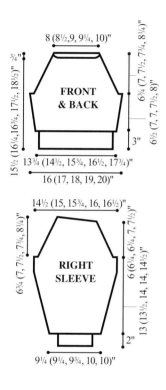

Norah Gaughan's sleeveless turtleneck with detachable cowl pairs casual elegance with cool comfort. Knit in a luxurious angora blend, it works up in flash in easy stockinette. Shown in size Small. The Sleeveless Cowlneck Top first appeared in the Fall '99 issue of *Vogue Knitting*.

Sleeveless Cowlneck Top

VERY EASY VERY VOGUE

SIZES
To fit Small (Medium, Large, X-Large). Directions are for smallest size with larger sizes in parentheses. If there is only one figure, it applies to all sizes.

KNITTED MEASUREMENTS
● Bust 34½ (37, 39, 42)"/87.5 (94, 99, 106.5)cm
● Length 23½ (24, 24½, 25)"/59.5 (61, 62, 63.5)cm

MATERIALS
● 7 (7, 7, 8) 1¾oz/50g balls (each approx 136yd/125m) of Reynolds/JCA *Chateau* (wool/nylon/angora 5) in #1 white
● One pair each sizes 11 and 13 (8 and 9mm) needles OR SIZE TO OBTAIN GAUGE

GAUGE
10 sts and 15 rows = 4"/10cm over St st using 2 strands of yarn and larger needles.
FOR PERFECT FIT, TAKE TIME TO CHECK GAUGE.

Note
Work with 2 strands of yarn held tog throughout.

BACK
With 2 strands of yarn, cast on 43 (46, 49, 52) sts. Work in St st until piece measures 5"/12.5cm from beg. **Dec row (RS)** K2, k2tog, k to last 4 sts, ssk, k2. Rep dec row every 6th row twice more—37 (40, 43, 46) sts. Work even until piece measures 11½"/29cm from beg. **Inc row (RS)** K2, M1, k to last 2 sts, M1, k2. Rep inc row every 6th row twice more—43 (46, 49, 52) sts. Work even until piece measures 15"/38cm from beg.

Armhole shaping
Dec row (RS) K2, k2tog, k to last 4 sts ssk, k2. Rep dec row every other row 3 (3, 4, 5) times more—35 (38, 39, 40) sts. Work even until armhole measures 7½ (8, 8½, 9)"/19 (20.5, 21.5, 23)cm.

Neck and shoulder shaping
Bind off 3 sts at beg of next 4 rows, 4 (5, 5, 5) sts at beg of next 2 rows, AT SAME TIME, bind off center 13 (14, 15, 16) sts and working both sides at once, dec 1 st from each neck edge every other row once.

FRONT
Work as for back until armhole measures 6 (6½, 7, 7½)"/15 (16.5, 18, 19)cm.

Neck shaping
Next row (RS) Work 13 (14, 14, 14) sts, join another double strand of yarn and bind off center 9 (10, 11, 12) sts, work to end. Working both sides at once, p 1 row. **Dec row (RS)** Work to last 4 sts of first side, ssk, k2; on 2nd side, k2, k2tog, k to end. Rep dec row every other row twice more, AT SAME TIME, when same length as back, shape shoulders by binding off 3 sts from each shoulder edge twice, 4 (5, 5, 5) sts once.

FINISHING
Block pieces lightly to measurements. Sew shoulder and side seams.

COWL COLLAR
With smaller needles and 2 strands of yarn, cast on 62 sts. Work in St st for 6"/15cm. Change to larger needles and cont in St st until piece measures 13"/33cm from beg. Bind off. Block lightly. Sew ends of rows tog to form side collar seam.

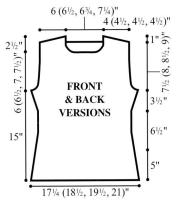

6 (6½, 6¾, 7¼)"
4 (4½, 4½, 4½)"
2½"
6 (6½, 7, 7½)"
1"
7½ (8, 8½, 9)"
3½"
6½"
15"
5"
FRONT & BACK VERSIONS
17¼ (18½, 19½, 21)"

Nancy Winarick uses fuzzy yarn to add a touch of texture to classic T-shirt styling. Sweet and sophisticated, this classic top is a cinch to stitch. Shown in size Small. The Short-Sleeved Top first appeared in the Fall '96 issue of *Vogue Knitting*.

Short-Sleeved Top

VERY EASY VERY VOGUE

SIZES
To fit X-Small (Small, Medium, Large). Directions are for smallest size with larger sizes in parentheses. If there is only one figure, it applies to all sizes.

KNITTED MEASUREMENTS
- Bust 31 (33, 35, 37, 39)"/79 (84, 89, 94, 99)cm
- Length 15¾ (16, 16, 17½, 18¼)"/40 (40.5, 40.5, 44.5, 46.5)cm
- Sleeve width at upper arm 16 (17, 17, 18, 19)"/40.5 (43, 43, 45.5, 48.5)cm
- Sleeve length to underarm 2 (2, 2, 3, 3)"/5 (5, 5, 7.5, 7.5)cm

MATERIALS
- 6 (7, 8, 9, 10) 1¾oz/50g of Silk City *Peluche* (viscose pile/nylon) in #10 butter
- One pair size 7 (4.5mm) needles OR SIZE TO OBTAIN GAUGE
- Stitch holders

GAUGE
21 sts and 28 rows to 4"/10 cm over St st. FOR PERFECT FIT, TAKE TIME TO CHECK GAUGE.

Notes
• Garment is worked in St st with the first st slipped knitwise on right side, slipped purlwise on wrong side.
• Peluche is a yarn with a directional nap. Work each side of neck separately using yarn as it comes off the cone.

BACK
Cast on 74 (78, 84, 90, 96) sts. Work in St st, inc 1 st each side every 1¼"/3cm 5 times—84 (88, 94, 100, 106) sts. Work even until piece measures 8 (8½, 8¼, 9, 9¼)"/20.5 (21.5, 21.5, 23, 24)cm from beg or desired length, ending with a WS row.

Armhole shaping
Bind off 4 sts at beg of next 2 rows. Dec 1 st each side every other row 2 (2, 3, 4, 5) times —72 (76, 80, 84, 88) sts. Work until armholes measures 7 (7¼, 7½, 7¾, 8)"/18 (18.5, 19, 19.5, 20.5)cm, ending with a WS row.

Neck and Shoulder Shaping
Right neck edge With RS facing, K 21 (23, 25, 27, 29) sts, put rem 51 (53, 55, 57, 59) sts on holder. Working one side only (do not work with 2 balls), dec 1 st at neck edge every other row twice. Work 2 more neck edge decs as established, AT THE SAME TIME shape shoulders, bind off from side edge 6 (6, 7, 8, 8) twice, 5 (7, 7, 7, 9) sts once. Left neck edge With RS facing, join yarn and bind off center 30 sts, k to end. Cont left neck edge decs and shoulder bindoffs as for left, reversing shaping.

FRONT
Work same as back until armhole measures 3 (3, 3¾ 2¾, 2¾, 2¾)"/cm, end with a WS row.

Neck shaping
Left neck edge (RS) K 29 (31, 33, 35, 37) sts, put rem 43 (45, 47, 49, 51) sts

on holder. Working one side at a time (do not work with 2 balls), bind off from neck edge 4 sts once, 3 sts once, then dec 1 st at neck edge every other row 5 times.

Left shoulder edge
When piece measures same as back, bind off from side edge 6 (6, 7, 8, 8) sts 2 times, 5 (7, 7, 7, 9) sts once.

Right neck and shoulder edge
With RS facing, join yarn and bind off center 14 sts, k to end. Cont right neck edge decs and shoulder bindoffs as for left, reversing shaping.

SLEEVES
Cast on 76 (78, 78, 82, 86) sts. Work in St st, inc 1 st each side every other row 5 (6, 6, 8, 9) times—86 (90, 90, 98, 104) sts. Work even until piece measures 2 (2, 2, 3, 3)"/5 (5, 5, 7.5, 7.5)cm from beg or desired length, end with a WS row.

Cap shaping
Bind off 4 sts at beg of next 2 rows. Dec 1 st each side every other row 3 (3, 3, 3, 4) times. Bind off 3 sts at beg of next 4 (4, 4, 6, 6) rows, 2 sts at beg of next 6 (8, 8, 8, 10) rows, 4 sts at beg of next 8 rows. Bind off rem 16 (16, 16, 18, 18) sts.

FINISHING
Sew shoulder seams. Set in sleeves. Sew side and sleeve seams.

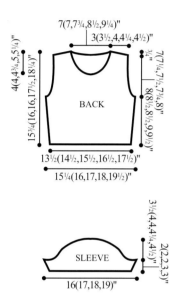

7(7,7¾,8½,9¼)"

3(3½,4,4¼,4½)"

¾"

7(7¼,7½,7¾,8)"

8(8½,8½,9,9½)"

4(4,4¾,5,5¼)"

BACK

15¾(16,16,17½,18¼)"

13½(14½,15½,16½,17½)"

15¼(16,17,18,19½)"

3½(4,4,4¼,4½)"

2(2,2,3,3)"

SLEEVE

16(17,18,19)"

Classic sweater shaping takes a romantic turn. Sheila Meyer's chic, simple style features modified set-in sleeves, a graceful raised neck and a scattering of applied knitted roses with embroidered leaves. Shown in size 36, the Pullover with Knitted Roses first appeared in the Holiday '88 issue of *Vogue Knitting*.

Pullover with Knitted Roses

VERY EASY VERY VOGUE

SIZES
To fit 32 (34, 36, 38, 40)"/81 (86, 91, 96, 101)cm bust. Directions are for smallest size with larger sizes in parentheses. If there is only one figure it applies to all sizes.

KNITTED MEASUREMENTS
● Bust 44 (46, 48, 50, 51½)"/ 110(114, 120, 124, 128)cm.
● Length 22 (23, 24, 24½, 25½)"/55 (58, 60, 61.5, 64)cm.
● Sleeve width at upper arm 18 (19, 20, 21, 22)"/45 (48, 50, 53, 55)cm.

MATERIALS
Original Yarn
● 12 (13, 14, 16, 18) 1¾oz/50g balls (each approx 93yd/85m) of Classic Elite *Boston* (wool 4) in #1955 celery (MC)
● 2 balls of #1927 burgundy (A)
● 1 ball of #1950 dark green (B)
Substitute Yarn
● 8 (9, 10, 11, 13) 1¾oz/50g balls (each approx 137yd/126m) of Classic Elite Yarns *Waterspun* (wool 4) in #5036 celery (MC)
● 2 balls of #5027 burgundy (A)
● 1 ball of #5015 dark green (B)
● One pair each sizes 5 and 7 (3.25 and 4.75mm) needles OR SIZE TO OBTAIN GAUGE

Note
The original yarn used for this sweater is no longer available. A comparable substitute has been made, which is available at the time of printing. Check gauge of substitute yarns very carefully before beginning.

GAUGE
20 sts and 28 rows to 4"/10cm over St st using size 7 (4.5mm) needles.
FOR PERFECT, TAKE TIME TO CHECK GAUGE.

BACK
With smaller needles and MC, cast on 110 (114, 118, 122, 126) sts. **Rib row 1** *K2, p2; rep from *, end k2. Rib row 2 *P2, k2; rep from *, end p2. Rep last 2 rows for 1 "/2.5cm, inc 0 (0, 2, 2, 2) sts evenly across last row—110 (114, 120, 124, 128) sts. Change to larger needles. Work in St st (k on RS, p on WS) until piece measures 12 (12½, 13, 13, 13½)"/30 (31.5, 32.5, 32.5, 34)cm from beg, end with a WS row.

Armhole shaping
Bind off 3 sts at beg of next 2 rows, 2 sts at beg of next 2 rows, then dec 1 st each side once—98 (102, 108, 112, 116) sts. Work even until armhole measures 9 (9½, 10, 10½, 11)"/22.5 (24, 25, 26.5, 27.5)cm, end with a WS row. Shoulder and neck shaping Bind off 12 sts at beg of next 2 rows, 10 (11, 12, 13, 13) sts at beg of next 2 rows, 10 (11, 12, 12, 13) sts at beg of next 2 rows, AT SAME TIME, bind off center 30 (30, 32, 34, 36) sts for neck and working both sides at once, dec 1 st at each neck edge every other row twice.

FRONT
Work as for back until armhole measures 7 (7½, 8, 8½, 9)"/17.5 (19, 20, 21.5, 22.5)cm, end with a WS row.

Neck shaping
Work across 43 (45, 47, 49, 51) sts, join 2nd ball of yarn and bind off 12 (12, 14, 14, 14) sts, work to end. Working both sides at once, bind off from each neck edge 3 sts once, 2 sts twice, then dec 1 st each side every other row 4 (4, 4, 5, 6) times, AT SAME TIME, when same length as back to shoulder, work shoulder shaping as for back.

SLEEVES
With smaller needles and MC, cast on 38 (38, 38, 42, 42) sts. Rib as for back for 1"/2.5cm. Change to larger needles. Work in St st, inc 1 st each side every other row 2 (4, 7, 7, 10) times, every 4th row 24 times—90 (94, 100, 104, 110) sts. Work even until piece measures 16 (16½, 17, 17, 17½)"/40 (41.5, 42.5, 42.5, 44)cm from beg.

Cap shaping
Bind off 3 sts from next 2 rows, 2 sts from next 2 rows, then dec 1 st each side every other row once. Bind off rem 78 (82, 88, 92, 98) sts,

FINISHING
Block pieces. Sew left shoulder seam.

Neckband
With RS facing, smaller needles and MC, beg at right shoulder, pick up and k 88 (88, 92, 96, 100) sts evenly around neck edge. Work in k2, p2 rib for 2"/5cm. Bind off in rib. Sew right shoulder seam, including neckband. Set in sleeves. Sew side and sleeve

seams.

Roses

With larger needles and A work assorted roses by casting on: 30 sts for small; 40 sts for medium; 60 sts for large. Work in k1, p1 rib for 2 rows. Bind off. Stitch roses to sweater randomly as foil: beg at center of rose, swirling piece to form rose. Embroider leaves in satin on either side of roses.

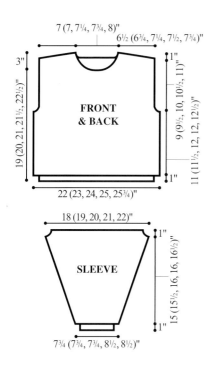

FRONT & BACK

7 (7, 7¼, 7¾, 8)"
6½ (6¾, 7¼, 7½, 7¾)"
3"
1"
19 (20, 21, 21½, 22½)"
9 (9½, 10, 10½, 11)"
11 (11½, 12, 12, 12½)"
1"
22 (23, 24, 25, 25¾)"

SLEEVE

18 (19, 20, 21, 22)"
1"
15 (15½, 16, 16, 16½)"
1"
7¾ (7¾, 7¾, 8½, 8½)"

Create a little evening drama in a chic ribbed capelet knit in winter white. Designed by Jean Guirguis, this ultra-sophisticated evening cover-up is shaped to the shoulder line with easy decreases. One size fits all. The Easy Capelet first appeared in the Winter '99/'00 issue of *Vogue Knitting*.

Easy Capelet

FOR INTERMEDIATE KNITTERS

SIZES
One size fits all.

KNITTED MEASUREMENTS
● Approx 48"/122cm wide by 17"/43cm long

MATERIALS
● 9 1¾oz/50g balls (each approx 90yd/83m) of Berroco, Inc. *Furz* (nylon/wool/acrylic 5) in #3801 white
● Size 7 (4.5mm) circular needle, 24"/60cm long OR SIZE TO OBTAIN GAUGE
● Stitch markers

GAUGES
• 22 sts and 28 rnds = 4"/10cm (slightly stretched) over k2, p2 rib using size 7 (4.5mm) needles.
• 20 sts = 4"/10cm (slightly stretched) over k2, p1 rib using size 7 (4.5mm) needles.
• 18 sts = 4"/10cm (slightly stretched) over k1, p1 rib using size 7 (4.5mm) needles.
FOR PERFECT FIT, TAKE TIME TO CHECK GAUGES.

BODY
Cast on 272 sts. Join, taking care not to twist sts on needle. Mark end of rnd and sl marker every rnd. Work in rnds of k2, p2 rib for 16"/40.5cm.

Shoulder shaping
Rnd 1 [K2, p2] twice, k2, pm, p2tog, k2, p2, k2, [p2tog, k2] 27 times, p2tog, k2, p2, k2, p2tog, pm, [k2, p2] twice, k2, pm, p2tog, k2, p2, k2, [p2tog, k2] 27 times, p2tog, k2 p2, k2, p2tog, pm—212 sts. **Rnd 2** and all even rnds Work even.

Rnds 3, 5, 7 and 9 Rib to next marker, sl marker, dec 1, rib to 2 sts before next marker, dec 1, sl marker, rib next marker, sl marker, dec 1, rib to 2 sts before next marker, dec 1—196 sts. **Rnd 11** *Rib to next marker, sl marker, dec 1, [p1, k2tog] 27 times, p1, rib to 2 sts before next marker, dec 1, sl marker; rep from * once more—138 sts. **Rnds 13 and 15** Rep rnd 3—130 sts. **Rnds 17 and 19** *[K2, p2tog] twice, k2, sl marker, dec 1, rib to 2 sts before next marker, dec 1, sl marker; rep from * once more—114sts. **Rnd 21** *[K2tog, p1] twice, k2tog, sl marker, dec 1, rib to 2 sts before next marker, dec 1, sl marker; rep from * once more—104 sts. **Rnd 23** Rep rnd 3—100 sts. Cont in k1, p1 rib for 4"/10cm. Bind off.

FINISHING
Block piece.

Soft, sensual and very romantic, Mari Lynn Patrick's flirty ballet top features all the right elements for sophistication. Accented with side ties, it knits up fast in easy garter stitch. Shown in size Small. The Surplice Wrap first appeared in the Fall '95 issue of *Vogue Knitting*.

Surplice Wrap

VERY EASY VERY VOGUE

SIZES
To fit Woman's Small (Medium, Large). Directions are for smallest size with larger sizes in parentheses. If there is only one figure, it applies to all sizes.

KNITTED MEASUREMENTS
● Bust at underarm (wrapped) 35 (37, 39½)"/89 (94, 100) cm
● Length 18 (18½, 19)"/45.5 (47, 48) cm
● Sleeve width at upperarm 11½ (12½, 13½)"/29 (32, 34) cm

MATERIALS
● 12 (13, 14) 1¾oz/50g skeins (each approx 61yd/54m) of GGH/Muench *Touch Me* (viscose/microfiber/new wool 5) in #3613 Dusty Rose
● One pair size 9 (5.5 mm) needles OR SIZE TO OBTAIN GAUGE

GAUGE
22 sts and 39 rows to 6"/15 cm over garter st using size 9 (5.5mm) needles. FOR PERFECT FIT, TAKE TIME TO CHECK GAUGE.

Note
This plush chenille yarn has a nap with a definite direction. When winding balls, beg with the same end of each skein of yarn to avoid shading of nap in knitted garment. To discourage worming, be sure to knit firmly and consistently. Avoid stopping in the middle of a row.

BACK
Cast on 58 (62, 66) sts. Work in garter st (k every row), inc 1 st each side every 2½"/6.5cm 3 times—64 (68, 72) sts. Work even until piece measures 9½"/24 cm from beg.

Armhole shaping
Bind off 3 sts at beg of next 2 rows. Dec 1 st each side every other row 3 times—52 (56, 60) sts. Work even until armhole measures 7½ (8, 8½)"/19 (20.5, 21.5) cm.

Shoulder and neck shaping
Bind off 5 sts at beg of next 6 (4, 0) rows, 6 sts at beg of next 0 (2, 6) rows, AT SAME TIME, bind off center 12 (14, 14) sts for neck, and working both sides at once, bind off from each neck edge 3 sts once and 2 sts once.

RIGHT FRONT
Cast on 51 (55, 59) sts. Work in garter st for 6 rows. **Next row (RS)** Cast on 67 sts, then loosely bind off these 67 sts (side tie), k to end. Cont in garter st, inc 1 st at end of RS rows every 2½"/6.5 cm (as for back) 3 times, AT SAME TIME, work 1 row even, then beg front edge shaping: **Next dec row (RS)** K2, k2tog, work to end. Rep dec row every 4th row 19 (18, 18) times more, then every other row 10 (14, 16) times, AT SAME TIME when same length as back to armhole, shape armhole (at beg of WS rows and end of RS rows) as for back. After all shaping is completed and there are 18 (19, 21) sts, work even until same length as back to shoulder, end with a RS row.

Shoulder shaping
Next row (WS) Bind off 5 (5, 6) sts (shoulder edge), work to end. Cont to bind off from shoulder edge 5 sts 2 (1, 0) times, 6 sts 0(1,2) times. Bind off remaining 3 sts for front band.

LEFT FRONT
Cast on and work as for right front for 5 rows.
Next row (WS) Cast on 133 sts, then loosely bind off these 133 sts (side tie), k to end. Work 2 rows even. Cont as for right front, reversing shaping by inc sts at beg of RS rows, and working front edge decs at end of RS rows as foll: Work to last 4 sts, k2tog, k2. Work armhole shaping at beg of RS rows. 3 sts rem after shoulder shaping. Place these sts on a holder.

SLEEVES
Cast on 24 (26, 28) sts. Work in garter st, inc 1 st each side every 12th (12th, 8th) row 6 (2, 3) times, every 10th row 3(8, 8) times—42 (46, 50) sts. Work even until piece measures 18"/45.5 cm from beg.

Cap shaping
Bind off 3 sts at beg of next 2 rows. Dec 1 st each side every other row 2 (4, 6) times, every 4th row twice, every 6th row twice. Bind off 1 st at beg of next 2 rows, 2 sts at beg of next 4 rows. Bind off rem 14 sts.

FINISHING
DO NOT BLOCK. Sew shoulder seams,

leaving 3 sts of front band unsewn. Pick up 3 sts from holder. Work even in garter st on these 3 sts until band fits across back neck to right shoulder. Bind off. Sew band in place along back neck. Sew edge seam of band. Set in sleeves. Sew right side seam, leaving opening ½"/1.5cm above lower edge to pull tie through. Sew right sleeve seam. Sew left side and sleeve seam.

4 (4½, 5)"
6 (6½, 6½)"
1"
18 (18½, 19)"
BACK
7½ (8, 8½)"
9½"
16 (17, 18)"
17½ (18½, 19¾)"

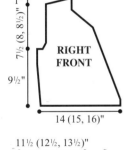

4¾ (5¼, 5¾)"
1"
7½ (8, 8½)"
RIGHT FRONT
9½"
14 (15, 16)"

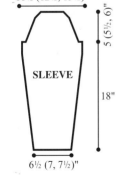

11½ (12½, 13½)"
5 (5½, 6)"
SLEEVE
18"
6½ (7, 7½)"

Something for Everyone

Wear-anywhere ease combined with a shot of sophistication and whimsy work for every member of the family.

Play multiple choice with this winning winter accessory. The ribbed rectangular tube, festooned with pompoms, can be worn as a hood or draped as a cowl. One size fits all. Designed by Lipp Holmfeld, the Ribbed Hooded Cowl first appeared in the Holiday '88 issue of *Vogue Knitting*.

Ribbed Hooded Cowl

VERY EASY VERY VOGUE

SIZES
One size fits all.

MATERIALS
Original Yarn
● 4 1¾oz/50g balls (each approx 126yd/115m) of Schoeller Wolle/Skacel Imports *Wollspass* (wool 3) in #6 fuchsia
Substitute Yarn
● 4 1¾oz/50g balls (each approx 131yd/120m) of Jaeger HandKnits *Baby Merino* (wool 2) in #219 red
● One pair size 4 (3.5mm) knitting needles OR SIZE TO OBTAIN GAUGE

Note
The original yarn used for this sweater is no longer available. A comparable substitute has been made, which is available at the time of printing. Check gauge of substitute yarns very carefully before beginning.

GAUGE
32 sts and 32 rows to 4"/10cm over k1, p1 rib using size 4 (3.5mm) needles. FOR PERFECT FIT, TAKE TIME TO CHECK GAUGE.

HAT
Cast on 165 sts. **Row 1 (RS)** *K1, p1; rep from *, end k1. **Row 2** *P1, k1; rep from *, end p1. Rep last 2 rows until piece measures 17"/43cm. Bind off knitwise.

FINISHING
Sew side seam to form a tube.

Pompoms
(make 7)
Cut two 2"/5cm cardboard circles. Cut hole in center approx 1/3 the size of circle. Cut ½"/1.5cm piece of circle away for easier wrapping of yarn. Place circles tog and wrap yarn thickly around circles. Insert scissors between cardboards and carefully cut around pompom. Cut a doubled strand and insert between cardboards. Tie tightly. Remove cardboards and trim pompom. Attach evenly around cast-on edge.

The weekend warrior steps out in style. Easy-to-execute moss stitch adds surface interest to a roomy crewneck pullover. Designed by Angela Bruton. Shown in size Medium. The Man's Moss-Stitched Pullover first appeared in the Fall '96 issue of *Vogue Knitting*.

Man's Moss-Stitched Pullover

VERY EASY VERY VOGUE

SIZES
To fit Small (Medium, Large). Directions are for smallest size with larger sizes in parentheses. If there is only one figure, it applies to all sizes.

KNITTED MEASUREMENTS
● Chest 45 (49, 53)"/114.5 (124.5, 134.5)cm.
● Length 27 (28, 29½)"/68.5 (71, 75)cm
● Sleeve width at upper arm 21 (22, 22½)" /53.5 (56, 58)cm
● Sleeve length to underarm 21 (22, 23)"/53.5 (65)cm

MATERIALS
● 10 (11, 12) 1¾oz/50g (each approx 109yd/ 99m) of Di Ve/Lane Borgosesia *Christine Melange* (mohair/ wool/acrylic 4) each in #1833 pale green (A) and #1832 pale blue (B).
● One pair size 11 (8mm) needles OR SIZE TO OBTAIN GAUGE
● Size 10 (6mm) circular needle16"/40cm long
● Stitch holders

GAUGE
12 sts and 18 rows to 4"/10 cm over St st and seed stitch.
FOR PERFECT FIT, TAKE TIME TO CHECK GAUGE.

Note
One strand of A with B held together throughout.

IRISH MOSS STITCH (MULTIPLE OF 2)
Rows 1 & 2 *K1, p1*; rep between *'s.
Rows 3 & 4 *P1, k1*; rep between *'s.
Rep rows 1-4 for pat.

BACK
With size 11 needles and one strand each of A and B, cast on 68 (74, 80) sts. Work in garter st (k every row) for 4 rows.
Beg Irish moss pat st (RS) with row 1, cont in pat until piece measures 16½ (17½, 18½)"/42 (44.5, 47.5)cm or desired length, end with WS row.

Armhole shaping
Bind off 3 sts at beg of next 2 rows, 1 sts at beg of next 4 rows—58 (64, 70) sts. Cont in pat until armhole measures 10½ (10½, 11)"/ 26.5 (26.5, 28)cm or desired length, end with WS row.

SHOULDER
Bind off 7 (8, 9) sts at beg of next 4 rows. Slip rem 30 (32, 34) sts onto holder.

FRONT
Work as for back until armhole measures 7½ (7½, 8)"/19 (19, 20.5)cm

Neck shaping
Work 18 (20, 22) sts in pat. Slip middle 22 (24, 26) stitches onto holder, join 2nd ball of yarn, work rem 18 (20, 22) sts. Working both sides at once, dec 1 st each neck edge every row, 4 times—14 (16,18) sts rem for each shoulder. Bind off shoulders as for back.

SLEEVE
With size 11 needles and 1 strand each of A and B, cast on 28 (28, 30 sts) sts. Work in garter st (Kevery row) for 4 rows.
Beg Irish moss pat st (RS) with row 1. Inc 1 st each side on next 2 rows. Cont in pat, inc 1 st each side every 4 rows 8 times; every 6 rows 9 times—66 (66, 68)sts. Work even until piece measures 21 (22, 22½)"/53.5 (56, 57.5)cm or desired length, end with a WS row.

Cap shaping
Bind off 3 (3, 4) sts at beg of next 2 rows. Dec 1 st each side every row 6 times.
***Row 1** K1, sl2, k1, pass the 2 slip sts over the k st (p2sso), work to last 4 sts, k3 tog k1.
Row 2 Dec 1 st each side.*
Rep between *'s twice—30 (30, 32) sts rem. Bind off all sts.

FINISHING
Sew shoulder seams. With RS facing, circular needle and 1 strand each of A and B, beg at left neck edge, pick up and k 8 sts at left neck edge, k 22 (24, 26) sts from holder, pick up and k 8 from right neck front edge, k 30 (32, 34) sts from holder—68 (72, 76) sts. Work k2, p2 rib for 3". Bind off loosely. Fold neckband rib in half to WS. Sew in place. Set in sleeves. Sew sleeve and side seams.

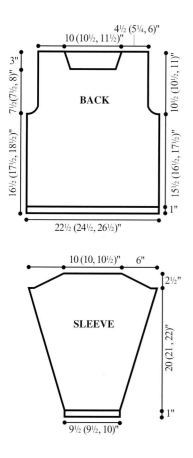

4½ (5¼, 6)"

10 (10½, 11½)"

3"

BACK

7½(7½, 8)"

10½ (10½, 11)"

16½ (17½, 18½)"

15½ (16½, 17½)"

1"

22½ (24½, 26½)"

10 (10, 10½)"   6"

2½"

SLEEVE

20 (21 , 22)"

1"

9½ (9½, 10)"

Chunky stitches and sporty styling hold up to rough and tumble play. Designed by Mari Lynn Patrick, this quick-knitting kids style is worked in ultra-easy reverse stockinette stitch. Shown in size 10. The Boy's Zip-Neck Pullover first appeared in the special Kids '01 issue of *Vogue Knitting*.

Boy's Zip-Neck Pullover

VERY EASY VERY VOGUE

SIZES
To fit 6 (8, 10, 12, 14).

KNITTED MEASUREMENTS
● Chest 36 (38, 40, 42, 44)"/91.5 (96.5, 101.5, 106.5, 111.5cm)
● Length 18½ (19½, 21, 22, 22½)"/47 (49.5, 53, 56, 57)cm
● Upper arm 14 (15, 16, 17, 18)"/35.5 (38, 40.5, 43, 45.5)cm

MATERIALS
Original Yarn
● 9 (10 , 10, 11, 12) 1¾oz/50g balls (each approx 55yd/50m) of Lane Borgosesia *Levante* (wool/nylon 5) in #252 grey
Substitute Yarn
● 4 (5, 5, 6, 6) 8oz/250g balls (each approx 132yd/121m) of Brown Sheep Co *Burly Spun* (wool 6) in #003 grey
● One pair size 11 (8mm) needles OR SIZE TO OBTAIN GAUGE
● One size 13 (9mm) needle for single-needle cast-on
● Size 11 (8mm) circular needle, 16"/40cm long
● 6"/15cm black neck zipper

Note
The original yarn used for this sweater is no longer available. A comparable substitute has been made, which is available at the time of printing. Check gauge of substitute yarns very carefully before beginning.

GAUGE
11 sts and 16 rows = 4"/10cm over reverse St st using size 11 (8mm) needles. FOR PERFECT FIT, TAKE TIME TO CHECK GAUGE.

BACK
With size 13 (9mm) needle, cast on 50 (52, 56, 58, 60) sts. Beg with a k row (WS row), work in reverse St st until piece measures 11 (12, 13½, 14½, 15)"/28 (30.5, 34, 37, 38)cm from beg.
Next row (RS) Knit. P next WS row (for ridge). Cont in reverse St st as before until piece measures 16½ (17½, 19, 20, 20½)"/42 (44.5, 48, 51, 52)cm from beg.

Shoulder shaping
Bind off 5 sts at beg of next 4 (6, 8, 6, 4) rows, 4 (4, 0, 6, 6) sts at beg of next 4 (2, 0, 2, 4) rows. Sl center 14 (14, 16, 16, 16) sts onto a holder for neck.

FRONT
Work as for back until piece measures 12½ (13½, 15, 16, 16½)"/32 (34, 38, 40.5, 42)cm and ridge is completed.

Separate for neck
Next row (RS) Work 24 (25, 27, 28, 29) sts, join another ball of yarn and bind off center 2 sts, work to end. Work both sides at once until placket measures 4"/10cm.

Neck shaping
On next row, sl 3 sts from each neck edge to holders for neck. Then cont to dec 1 st from each neck edge every

other row 3 (3, 4, 4, 4) times, AT SAME TIME, when same length as back, bind off 5 sts from each shoulder edge 2 (3, 4, 3, 2) times, 4 (4, 0, 6, 6) sts 2 (1, 0, 1, 2) times.

SLEEVES
With size 13 (9mm) needles, cast on 24 (26, 28, 28, 30) sts. Beg with a k row (WS row), work in reverse St st, inc 1 st each side every 6th row 7 (8, 8, 9, 10) times—38 (42, 44, 46, 50) sts. Work even until piece measures 12 (13, 14½, 16, 17)"/30.5 (33, 37, 40.5, 43)cm from beg. K1 row on RS for ridge. Bind off purlwise.

FINISHING
Block pieces to measurements. Sew shoulder seams.

Collar
With circular needle, pick up and k 40 (40, 44, 44, 44) sts evenly around neck edge. K1 row on WS for ridge. Beg with a k row, work in St st for 2"/5cm. Bind off loosely. Place markers at 7 (7½, 8, 8½, 9)"/18 (19, 20.5, 21.5, 23)cm down from shoulders for armholes. Sew sleeves to armholes between markers. Sew side and sleeve seams. With circular needle, pick up and k 20 sts along one side of collar and placket, 2 sts at center and 20 sts along other side. Bind off knitwise. Sew zipper to placket opening.

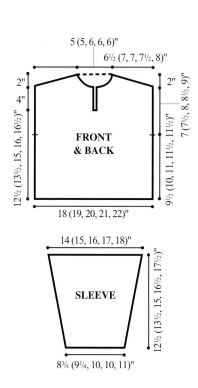

5 (5, 6, 6, 6)"

6½ (7, 7, 7½, 8)"

2"

4"

12½ (13½, 15, 16, 16½)"

FRONT & BACK

2"

7 (7½, 8, 8½, 9)"

9½ (10, 11, 11½, 11½)"

18 (19, 20, 21, 22)"

14 (15, 16, 17, 18)"

SLEEVE

12½ (13½, 15, 16½, 17½)"

8¾ (9¼, 10, 10, 11)"

Kick back and relax in his-and-hers V-neck pullovers (Woman's version shown on page 142). An easy basketweave stitch adds delightful textural interest. Shown in size Medium. The Man's Basketweave pullover first appeared in the Spring/Summer '97 issue of *Vogue Knitting*.

Man's Basketweave Pullover

VERY EASY VERY VOGUE

SIZES
To fit Small (Medium, Large, X-Large). Directions are for smallest size with larger sizes in parentheses. If there is only one figure, it applies to all sizes.

KNITTED MEASUREMENTS
● Chest 46 (48, 50, 52)"/117 (122, 127, 132)cm
● Length 27½ (28, 28½, 29)"/70 (71, 72.5, 73.5)cm
● Sleeve width at upper arm 17 (18, 19½, 21)"/ 43 (45.5, 49.5, 53)cm

MATERIALS
Original Yarn
● 15 (15, 16, 18) 1¾oz/50g skeins (each approx 84yd/77m) of Berroco *Cotton 100* (cotton 5) in #9104 khaki
Substitute Yarn
● 115 (15, 16, 18) 1¾oz/50g (each approx 84yd/77m) of Mission Falls/Unique Kolours *1824 Cotton* (cotton 4) in #300 lichen
● One pair each sizes 6 and 8 (4 and 5mm) needles OR SIZE TO OBTAIN GAUGE

Note
The original yarn used for this sweater is no longer available. A comparable substitute has been made, which is available at the time of printing. Check gauge of substitute yarns very carefully before beginning.

GAUGE
316 sts and 25 rows to 4"/10cm over pat st using larger needles.

FOR PERFECT FIT, TAKE TIME TO CHECK GAUGE.

BACK
With smaller needles, cast on 92 (96, 100, 104) sts. **Row 1 (RS)** *K4, p4; rep from * to end. Row 2 K the knit and p the purl sts. Cont in k4, p4 rib until piece measures 1"/2.5cm from beg, end with a RS row. Change to larger needles and work in St st for 4 rows. *Next row (RS) K0 (0, 2, 2), work 24 sts of chart pat, [k10 (12, 12, 14), work 24-st chart pat] twice, k0 (0, 2, 2). Cont in this way through row 24 of chart. Work 8 rows in St st. **Next row (RS)** K17 (18, 20, 21), work 24-st chart pat, k10 (12, 12, 14), work 24-st chart pat, k to end. Cont in this way through row 24 of chart. Work 8 rows in St st.* Rep between *'s for pat st until piece measures 18"/45.5cm from beg, end with a WS row.

Armhole shaping
Keeping pat, bind off 3 (3, 4, 4) sts at beg of next 2 rows, 2 sts at beg of next 2 (2, 2, 4) rows, 1 st at beg of next 8 (8, 8, 6) rows—74 (78, 80, 82) sts. Work even until armhole measures 8½ (9, 9½, 10)"/21.5 (23, 24, 25.5)cm, end with a WS row.

Neck and shoulder shaping
Bind off 8 sts from each shoulder edge 3 (2, 2, 2) times, 9 sts 0 (1, 1, 1) time and AT SAME TIME, join 2nd ball of yarn and bind off center 18 (20, 22, 24) sts and working both sides at once, bind off 2 sts from each neck edge twice.

FRONT
Work as for back until armhole mea-

sures 1½ (2, 2½, 3)"/4 (5, 6.5, 7.5)cm, end with a WS row.

V-neck shaping
Next row (RS) Work to 2 sts before center (of center block), dec 1 st, join 2nd skein of yarn and dec 1 st, work to end. Working both sides at once, dec 1 st each neck edge every 2nd row 2 (4, 6, 9) times more, every 4th row 10 (9, 8, 6) times—24 (25, 25, 25) sts rem each side. When same length as back, shape shoulders as for back.

SLEEVES
With smaller needles, cast on 46 sts. **Row 1 (RS)** K1, *k4, p4; rep from * end k5. Cont in k4, p4 rib as established until piece measures 1"/2.5cm from beg, inc 2 (2, 4, 4) sts across last WS row—48 (48, 50, 50) sts. Change to larger needles and work in St st for 2 rows. Inc 1 st each side of next row. P 1 row. **Next row (RS)** K 13 (13, 14, 14), work 24 sts of chart pat, k to end. Cont to work alternating pat st as on back with 10 (12, 12, 14) sts between each block pat, AT THE SAME TIME, inc 1 st each side every 10th (10th, 8th, 8th) row 9 (11, 13, 16) times—68 (72, 78, 84) sts. Work even until piece measures 19½ (20, 21, 22)"/49.5 (50.5, 53, 56)cm from beg.

Cap shaping
Work as for back armhole. Bind off rem 50 (54, 58, 62) sts.

FINISHING
Block pieces lightly. Sew left shoulder seam. With smaller needles, pick up and k 36 sts from back neck, 36 sts

from left v-neck, place marker (pm), 36sts from right v-neck. **Row 1 (WS)** P4, *k4, p4; rep from * to marker, then p4, k4 to end. **Row 2 (RS)** Rib to 2 sts before marker, k2tog, sl marker, ssk, rib to end. Rep row 2 every 2nd row 3 times more. Bind off in rib. Sew right shoulder and neckband seam. Set sleeves into armholes. Sew side and sleeve seams.

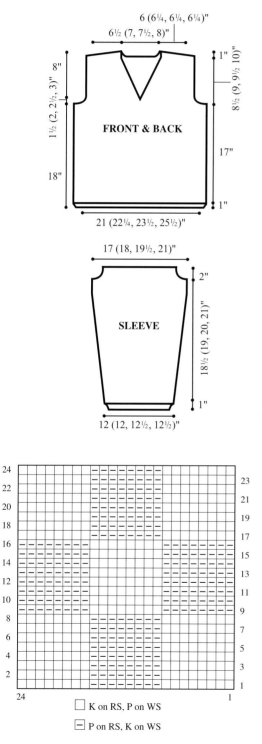

6 (6¼, 6¼, 6¼)"

6½ (7, 7½, 8)"

8"

1½ (2, 2½, 3)"

FRONT & BACK

18"

1"

8½ (9, 9½ 10)"

17"

1"

21 (22¼, 23½, 25½)"

17 (18, 19½, 21)"

2"

SLEEVE

18½ (19, 20, 21)"

1"

12 (12, 12½, 12½)"

☐ K on RS, P on WS

☐ P on RS, K on WS

A cozy woman's basketweave pullover complements a man's version shown on page 140. A simple basketweave stitch lends texture to this weekend staple, the relaxed fit provides comfort all day long. Shown in size Medium. The Woman's Basketweave Pullover first appeared in the Spring/Summer '97 issue of *Vogue Knitting*.

Woman's Basketweave Pullover

VERY EASY VERY VOGUE

SIZES
To fit Small (Medium, Large). Directions are for smallest size with larger sizes in parentheses. If there is only one figure it applies to all sizes.

KNITTED MEASUREMENTS
● Bust 46 (49, 53)"/117 (124, 134.5)cm
● Length 20 (20½, 21)"/50.5 (52, 53)cm
● Sleeve width at upper arm 15½ (16, 17½)"/ 39.5 (40.5, 44.5)cm

MATERIALS
● 13 (14, 15) 1¾oz/50g (each approx 75yd/ 69m) of Berroco *Glacé* (rayon 4) in #2730 stone
● One pair each sizes 6 and 8 (4 and 5mm) needles OR SIZE TO OBTAIN GAUGE

GAUGE
18 sts and 27 rows to 4"/10cm over pat st using larger needles.
FOR PERFECT FIT, TAKE TIME TO CHECK GAUGE.

BACK
With smaller needles, cast on 104 (112, 120) sts. **Row 1 (RS)** *K4, p4; rep from * to end. **Row 2** K the knit and p the purl sts. Cont in k4, p4 rib for 2 more rows. Change to larger needles and work in St st for 4 rows. ***Next row (RS)** K10 (14, 18), work 12-st chart pat, [k6, work 12-st chart pat] 4 times, k 10 (14, 18). Cont in this way through row 12 of chart. Work 4 rows in St st. **Next Row (RS)** K0 (2, 6), beg with st 3 (1, 1) of chart, work to end of chart, [k6, work 12-st chart pat] 5 times ending last rep with 10th st of chart (k2, k6). Cont in this way through row 12 of chart. Work 4 rows in St st. *Rep between *'s for pat st until piece measures 11½"/29cm from beg, end with a WS row.

Armhole shaping
Keeping pat, bind off 3 sts at beg of next 2 rows, 2 sts at beg of next 2 (2, 4) rows, dec 1 st each side every 2nd row 5 (6, 5) times—84 (90, 96) sts. Work even until armhole measures 7½ (8, 8½)"/19 (20.5, 21.5)cm, end with a WS row.

Neck and shoulder shaping
Bind off 9 (10, 10) sts from each shoulder edge twice, 8 (9, 11) sts once and AT SAME TIME, bind off center 24 (24, 26) sts and working both sides at once, bind off 2 sts from each neck edge twice.

FRONT
Work as for back until armhole measures 3½ (4, 4½)"/9 (10, 11.5)cm, end with a WS row.

V-neck shaping
Next row (RS) Work 40 (43, 46) sts, dec 1 st, join 2nd ball of yarn and dec 1 st, work to end. Working both sides at once, dec 1 st each neck edge every 2nd row 15 (15, 16) times more—26 (29, 31) sts rem each side. When same length as back, shape shoulder as for back.

SLEEVES
With smaller needles, cast on 40 sts. Work in k4, p4 rib until piece measures 1"/2.5cm from beg, inc 2 (2, 4) sts across last WS row—42 (42, 44) sts. Change to larger needles and work in St st for 4 rows. **Next Row (RS)** K15 (15, 16), work 12 sts of chart pat, k to end. Cont to work alternating pat st as on back (adding chart pats outwards as sts inc), AT SAME TIME, inc 1 st each side every 6th row 7 (11, 17) times, every 8th row 7 (4, 0) times—70 (72, 78) sts. Work even until piece measures 16½"/42cm from beg.

Cap shaping
Work as for back armhole. Bind off rem 50 (50, 54)sts.

FINISHING
Block pieces lightly. Sew left shoulder seam. With smaller needles pick up and k 36 sts from back neck, 28 sts from left V-neck, place marker, 28 sts from right V-neck. **Row 1 (WS)** P4, *k4, p4; rep from * to marker then p4, k4, to end. **Row 2 (RS)** Rib to 2 sts before marker, k2tog , sl marker, ssk, rib to end. Rep row 2 every 2nd row 3 times more. Bind off in rib. Sew right shoulder and neck band seam. Set sleeves into armholes. Sew side and sleeve seams.

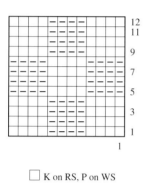

□ K on RS, P on WS

− P on RS, K on WS

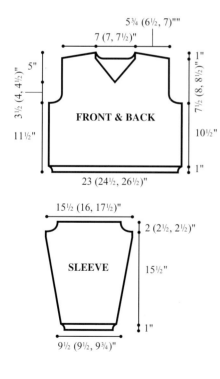

5¾ (6½, 7)""""

7 (7, 7½)"

5"

3½ (4, 4½)"

1"

7½ (8, 8½)"

FRONT & BACK

11½"

10½"

1"

23 (24½, 26½)"

15½ (16, 17½)"

2 (2½, 2½)"

SLEEVE

15½"

1"

9½ (9½, 9¾)"

Get graphic with a striking black and beige pattern. Designed for both men and women, Lily Chin's classic dropped-shoulder crewneck sweater stands out in a crowd. Shown in size 40. The Arrowhead Pullover first appeared in the Spring/Summer '88 issue of *Vogue Knitting*.

Arrowhead Pullover

VERY EASY VERY VOGUE

SIZES

To fit man's or woman's 32 (34, 36, 38, 40, 42, 44)"/81 (86, 91, 96, 101, 106, 112)cm bust/chest. Directions are for smallest size with larger sizes in parentheses. If there is only one set of figures it applies to all sizes.

KNITTED MEASUREMENTS

● Bust/Chest measurement at underarm 40 (42, 44, 46, 48, 49½, 52)"/100 (106, 111, 115, 120, 124, 129)cm.

● Length 23½ (24½, 25, 26, 26½, 27, 27½)"/59.5 (61.5, 63, 65, 67, 68, 69)cm.

● Sleeve width at upper arm 18 (19, 19, 20, 20, 21, 21)"/46 (48, 48, 51, 51, 53, 53)cm.

MATERIALS

Original Yarn

● 11 (11, 12, 12, 13, 13, 14) 1¾oz/50g balls (each approx 93yd/85m) of Phildar *Coton D'Egypte* 4½ (cotton 4) in #67 black (MC)

● 9 (9, 9, 10, 10, 10, 11) balls #8 beige (CC)

Substitute Yarn

● 10 (10, 11, 11, 11, 11, 12) 1¾oz/50g balls (each approx 110yd/101m) of Ornaghi Filati/Trendsetter *Elba* (cotton 3) in #002 black

● 8 (8, 8, 9, 9, 9) balls #12 ecru

● One pair each sizes 5 and 7 (3.75 and 4.5mm) needles OR SIZE TO OBTAIN GAUGE

● Size 5 (3.75mm) circular needle 16"/40cm

Note

The original yarn used for this sweater is no longer available. A comparable substitute has been made, which is available at the time of printing. Check gauge of substitute yarns very carefully before beginning.

GAUGE

322 sts and 24 rows to 4"/10cm over chart pat using size 7 (4.5mm) needles. FOR PERFECT FIT, TAKE TIME TO CHECK GAUGE.

Note

When changing colors, twist yarns on WS to prevent holes and carry yarn not in use loosely across back of work. Weave or twist yarns not in use around working yarn every 3 or 4 sts.

BACK

With smaller needles and MC, cast on 92 (98, 102,106, 110, 114,118) sts. **Twisted rib row 1** *K1 tbl, p1; rep from * to end. Rep last row for 3"/7.5, inc 18 (18, 20, 20, 22, 22, 24) sts evenly across last row—110 (116, 122, 126, 132, 136, 142) sts. Change to larger needles. Beg as indicated work in chart pat for desired version until piece measures 23½ (24½, 25, 26, 26½, 27, 27½)"/59.5 (61.5, 63, 65, 67, 68, 69)cm from beg. Bind off.

FRONT

Work as for back until piece measures 20½ (21½, 22, 23, 23½, 24, 24½)"/52 (54, 55.5, 57.5, 59.5, 60.5, 61.5)cm from beg, end with a WS row.

Neck shaping

Next row (RS) Work 46 (49, 51, 52, 54, 55, 59) sts, join 2nd ball of yarn and bind off 18 (18, 20, 22, 24, 26, 24) sts, work to end. Working both sides at once, bind off from each neck edge 2 sts 2 (2, 2, 2, 2, 2, 3) times, dec 1 st every row 6 times. When same length as back, bind off rem 36 (39, 41, 42, 44, 45, 47) sts each side.

SLEEVES

With smaller needles and MC, cast on 48 (48, 48, 48, 50, 52, 52) sts. Work in twisted rib as for back for 3"/7.5cm, inc 12 (12, 14, 14, 14, 14, 14) sts evenly across last row—60 (60, 62, 62, 64, 66, 66) sts. Change to larger needles. Beg with 4th (4th, 3rd, 3rd, 2nd, 1st, 1st) st of chart, work in chart pat for desired version, AT SAME TIME, inc 1 st each end (working inc sts into chart pat) every 4th row 18 (21, 18, 24, 21, 24, 23) times, every 6th row 2 (1, 3, 0, 2, 1, 2) times—100 (104, 104, 110, 110, 116, 116) sts. Work even in pat until piece measures 18 (18½, 18½, 19½, 20, 21, 21½)"/45 (46.5, 46.5, 49.5, 50, 52.5, 54)cm from beg. Bind off.

FINISHING

Block pieces. Sew shoulder seams.

Neckband

With RS facing, circular needle and MC, pick up and k102 (102, 106, 112, 116, 124, 128) sts evenly around entire neck edge. Join and work in rnds of twisted rib as foll: **Rnd 1** *K1 tbl, p1: rep from * around. **Rnd 2** *K1, p1 tbl; rep from * around. Rep rnds 1 and 2 for 1"/2.5cm.

P next rnd (turning ridge). Cont in twisted rib for 1"/2.5cm more. Bind off in rib. Fold at turning ridge and sew to WS. Place markers 9 [9½, 9½, 10, 10, 10½, 10½)"/23 (24, 24, 25.5, 25.5, 26.5, 26.5)cm down from shoulders on front and back for armholes. Sew top of sleeves between markers. Sew side and sleeve seams.

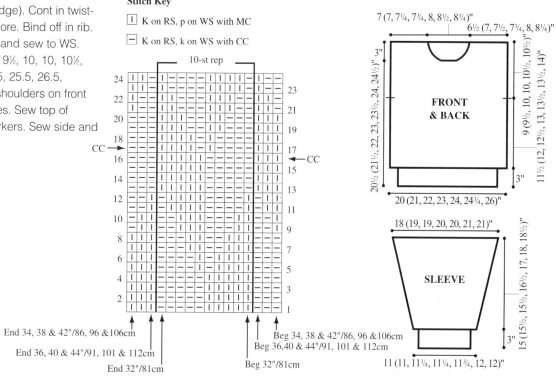

Stitch Key

☐ K on RS, p on WS with MC

— K on RS, k on WS with CC

10-st rep

CC →

← CC

End 34, 38 & 42"/86, 96 &106cm

End 36, 40 & 44"/91, 101 & 112cm

End 32"/81cm

Beg 34, 38 & 42"/86, 96 &106cm

Beg 36,40 & 44"/91, 101 & 112cm

Beg 32"/81cm

7 (7, 7¼, 7¾, 8, 8½, 8¾)"

6½ (7, 7½, 7¾, 8, 8¼)"

3"

FRONT & BACK

9 (9½, 10, 10, 10½, 10½)"

20½ (21½, 22, 23, 23½, 24, 24½)"

11½ (12, 12½, 13, 13½, 13½, 14)"

20 (21, 22, 23, 24, 24¾, 26)"

3"

18 (19, 19, 20, 20, 21, 21)"

SLEEVE

15 (15½, 15½, 16½, 17, 18, 18½)"

3"

11 (11, 11¼, 11¼, 11¾, 12, 12)"

Melissa Leapman uses muted stripes and rugged ribbing to put a modern spin on the traditional V-neck pullover. Worked in warm wool, it's a natural for work or play. Shown in size Medium. The Man's Striped Pullover first appeared in the Fall '96 issue of *Vogue Knitting*.

Man's Striped Pullover

VERY EASY VERY VOGUE

SIZES
To fit Small (Medium, Large). Directions are for smallest size with larger sizes in parentheses. If there is only one figure, it applies to all sizes.

KNITTED MEASUREMENTS
● Chest 47 (49, 50½)"/119.5 (124.5, 128.5)cm
● Length 25 (26, 27)"/63.5 (66, 68.5)cm
● Sleeve width at upper arm 18 (19, 20)"/46 (48.5, 51)cm
● Length 27 (27½, 27½)"/68.5 (70, 70)cm
● Sleeve length to underarm 21 (21, 22½)"/ 53.5 (53.5, 57.5)cm

MATERIALS
● 5 (5, 7) 1¾oz/50g balls (each approx 109 yds/99m) of Reynolds/JCA *Lite-Lopi* (wool 4)in #414 oxblood (A)
● 3 (4, 5) each in #427 siena brown and #426 gold moss
● One pair size 8 (5mm) needles OR SIZE TO OBTAIN GAUGE
● Size 8 (5.mm) circular needle 16"/40cm long.
● Stitch holders

GAUGE
18 sts and 22 rows to 4"/10cm over St st. FOR PERFECT FIT, TAKE TIME TO CHECK GAUGE.

Stitch glossary
Stripe sequence pat (even # of sts)

Row 1 (RS) *K1 with A, k1 with B*; rep between *'s.
Row 2 (WS) *P1 with A, p1 with B*; rep between *'s.
Rows 3-12 With B, work in St st. **Row 13** *K1 with B, k1 with C*, rep between *'s. Row 14 *P1 with B, p1 with C*; rep between *'s.
Rows 15-24 With C, work in St st. **Row 25** *K1 with C, k1 with A*; rep between *'s.
Row 26 * P1 with C, p1 with A*; rep between *'s.
Rows 27-36 With A, work in St st. Rep rows 1-36 for stripe pat.

BACK
With A, cast on 106 (110, 114) sts. Work in k2, p2 rib for 2½"/6cm, end with a WS row.
Next row (RS) K. **Next row (WS)** P. **Beg stripe sequence pat (RS)** Work rows stripe sequence 1-36, rep sequence until piece measures 24 (25, 26)"/61 (63.5, 66)cm from beg, end with a WS row.

Shoulder shaping
Bind off 12 (13, 13) sts at beg of next 4 rows, 12 (12, 14) sts at beg of next 2 rows. Sl rem 34 sts to a holder for back neck.

FRONT
Work as for back until piece measures 17½ (18½, 19½)"/44.5 (47, 49.5)cm from beg, end with a WS row.

V-neck and shoulder shaping
Next row (RS): Work across 51 (53, 55) sts, k2tog, join 2nd ball of yarn, ssk, work to end. Working both sides at once, dec 1 st at each neck edge every

other row 13 times more, then every 4th row 3 times. AT THE SAME TIME, when front measures same as back to shoulders bind off from each shoulder edge 12 (13, 13) sts twice, 12 (12, 14) sts once.

SLEEVES
With A, cast on 50 sts. Work in k2, p2 rib for 1¼/3cm, end with a WS row.
Next row (RS) K.
Next row (WS) Beg stripe sequence pat Work rows stripe sequence 1-36, rep sequence until piece measures 21 (21, 22½)"/53.5 (53.5, 57.5)cm or desired length from beg. AT SAME TIME inc 1 st each side of row 1 of stripe sequence, then every 6th row 15 (17, 19) times—82 (86, 90) sts. Work even Bind off all sts.

FINISHING
Sew shoulder seams.

V-neck band
With RS facing, using circular needle and A, beg at left shoulder neck edge, pick up and k 40 sts evenly along left front neck to center front, place marker, 40 sts evenly along right front neck, 34 sts from back neck holder—114 sts. First rnd Work in p2, k2 rib to 2 sts before center marker, ssk, sl center marker, k2tog, work in p2, k2 rib to end. Cont in est rib decreasing 1 st before and after marker every row. When neckband measures 1½"/3.5cm from beg, bind off in pat. Place markers 9 (9½,10)"/23 (24, 25.5)cm down from shoulder seams on front and back for armholes. Sew top of sleeves between markers. Sew side and sleeve seams.

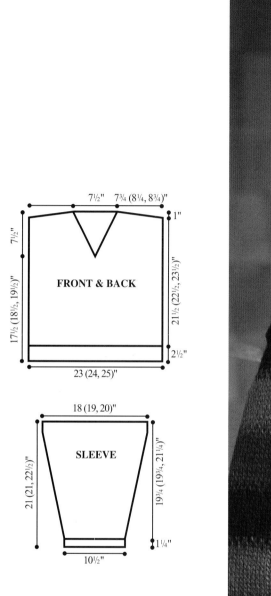

FRONT & BACK

7½"   7¾ (8¼, 8¾)"   1"

7½"

17½ (18½, 19½)"   21½ (22½, 23½)"

2½"

23 (24, 25)"

SLEEVE

18 (19, 20)"

21 (21, 22½)"   19¾ (19¾, 21¼)"

1¼"

10½"

Strands of black and white yarn held together create the striking tweedy effect on this easy-to-knit pullover. Designed by Carla Scott, it's sure to become one of his all-time favorites. Shown in size 10. The Boy's Rolled-Neck Pullover first appeared in the Special Kids '01 issue of *Vogue Knitting*.

Boy's Rolled-Neck Pullover

VERY EASY VERY VOGUE

SIZES
To fit 10 (12, 14).

KNITTED MEASUREMENTS
● Chest 35 (36, 38)"/89 (91.5, 96.5)cm
● Length 21 (22, 23)"/53 (56, 58.5)cm
● Upper arm 16 (17, 18)"/40.5 (43, 45.5)cm

MATERIALS
● 4 5oz/250g balls (each approx 525yd/472m) of Wool Pak Yarns NZ/Baabajoe's Wool Co. *8 Ply* (wool 4) each in #10 black (A) and #01 natural (B)
● One pair each sizes 10 and 10½ (6 and 6.5mm) needles OR SIZE TO OBTAIN GAUGE
● Sizes 10 and 10½ (6 and 6.5mm) circular needles, 16"/40cm long
● Stitch holders

GAUGE
14 sts and 18 rows = 4"/10cm over St st using larger needles.
FOR PERFECT FIT, TAKE TIME TO CHECK GAUGE.

NOTE
Work with 1 strand of A and B held tog throughout.

BACK
With smaller needles and 1 strand of A and B held tog, cast on 62 (64, 66) sts. Work in k2, p2 rib for 2"/5cm. Change to larger needles and work in St st until piece measures 21 (22, 23)"/53 (56, 58.5)cm from beg. Bind off.

FRONT
Work as for back until piece measures 18½ (19½, 20½)"/47 (49.5, 52)cm from beg.

Neck shaping
K25 (26, 26), place center 12 (12, 14) sts on a holder, join a 2nd ball of yarn and work to end. Working both sides at once, bind off at neck edge 3 sts once, 2 sts once, then dec 1 (0, 0) sts each neck edge once—19 (21, 21) sts each side. Work even until same length as back. Bind off sts each side for shoulders.

SLEEVES
With smaller needles and 1 strand of A and B held tog, cast on 26 (26, 28) sts. Work in k2, p2 rib for 2"/5cm. Change to larger needles and work in St st, inc 1 st each side every other row 10 (12, 13) times, every 4th row 5 times—56 (60, 64) sts. Work even until piece measures 11½ (12, 13)"/29 (30.5, 33)cm from beg, inc 10 sts evenly spaced across last WS row—66 (70, 74) sts. Change to smaller needles and work in k2, p2 rib for 4"/10cm. Bind off loosely in rib.

FINISHING
Block pieces to measurements. Sew shoulder seams.

Turtleneck
With RS facing, smaller circular needle and 1 strand of A and B held tog, pick up and k60 (60, 64) sts evenly around neck, working across sts from front holder. Join and work in rnds of k2, p2 rib for 2"/5cm. Change to larger circular needle and work in rnds of St st for 1½"/4cm. Bind off. Place markers 8 (8½, 9)"/20.5 (21.5, 23)cm down from shoulder seams. Set in sleeves between markers. Sew side and sleeve seams.

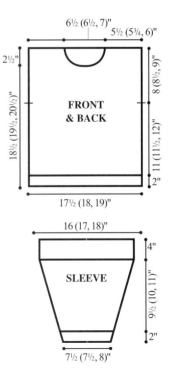

Schematic measurements — FRONT & BACK: 6½ (6½, 7)"; 5½ (5¾, 6)"; 2½"; 8 (8½, 9)"; 18½ (19½, 20½)"; 11 (11½, 12)"; 2"; 17½ (18, 19)". SLEEVE: 16 (17, 18)"; 4"; 9½ (10, 11)"; 2"; 7½ (7½, 8)".

This ribbed hat with gathered drawstring top and whimsical pompom trim is a cinch to knit. Designed by Lipp Holmfeld, this easy first-time project makes a playful accent to any casual ensemble. One size fits all. The Ribbed Drawstring Hat first appeared in the Holiday '88 issue of *Vogue Knitting*.

Ribbed Drawstring Hat

VERY EASY VERY VOGUE

SIZES
One size fits all.

MATERIALS
Original Yarn
● 3 1¾oz/50g balls (each approx 140yd/128m) of Pingouin 4 *Pingouins* (wool 3) in #69 lime green

Substitute Yarn
● 3 1¾oz/50g balls (each approx 176yd/162m) of Koigu Wool Designs *Premium Merino* (wool 2) in #2132 br green
● One pair size 4 (3.5mm) knitting needles OR SIZE TO OBTAIN GAUGE

Note
The original yarn used for this sweater is no longer available. A comparable substitute has been made, which is available at the time of printing. Check gauge of substitute yarns very carefully before beginning.

GAUGE
36 sts and 34 rows to 4"/10cm over k1, p1 rib (unstretched) using size 4 (3.5mm) needles.
FOR PERFECT FIT, TAKE TIME TO CHECK GAUGE.

HAT
Cast on 157 sts. **Row 1 (RS)** *K1, p1; rep from *, end k1.
Row 2 *P1, k1; rep from * end p1. Rep last 2 rows for 14"/35.5cm.
Next row (RS) K1, *rib 3 sts, k2tog; rep from * end k1—126 sts.
Eyelet row P1, *yo, ribs, yo, ribs; rep from *, end ribs—156 sts. Bind off knitwise.

FINISHING
Sew side seam. Cut a strand 3yds/3m long and make a twisted cord. Thread cord through eyelet row and tie tightly. Make two pompoms and attach to end of cord.

For weekend wear or causal Fridays, a textural turtleneck is the way to go. Designed by Norah Gaughan, this chunky pullover gets subtle surface interest from knit-and-purl diamonds. Shown in size Large. The Man's Turtleneck Pullover first appeared in the Winter '00/'01 issue of *Vogue Knitting*.

Man's Turtleneck Pullover

VERY EASY VERY VOGUE

SIZES
To fit Man's Small (Medium, Large, X-Large, XX-Large). Directions are for smallest size with larger sizes in parentheses. If there is only one figure, it applies to all sizes.

KNITTED MEASUREMENTS
● Chest 42 (45, 48, 51, 54)"/106.5 (114, 122, 129.5, 137)cm
● Length 26½ (27, 27½, 28, 28½)"/67 (68.5, 70, 71, 72.5)cm
● Upper arm 20¼ (21, 21½, 22, 22½)"/51 (53, 54, 56, 57)cm

MATERIALS
● 16 (17, 18, 20, 21) 1¾oz/50g hanks (each approx 82yd/74m) of Reynolds/JCA *Contessa* (wool/angora/polyamide 5) in #62 dk green
● One pair size 10 (6mm) needles OR SIZE TO OBTAIN GAUGE
● Stitch holders

GAUGE
14 sts and 20 rows = 4"/10cm over St st using size 10 (6mm) needle.
FOR PERFECT FIT, TAKE TIME TO CHECK GAUGE.

BACK
Cast on 73 (79, 85, 89, 95) sts.

Beg chart pat
Row 1 (RS) Beg with st 16 (13, 10, 8, 5), work to rep line, then work 20-st rep ending with st 28 (31, 34, 36, 39). Cont to foll chart in this way through row 38, then rep rows 39-60 twice, then discontinue chart and cont in St st only until piece measures 25½ (26, 26½, 27, 27½)"/65 (66, 67, 68.5, 70)cm from beg.

Shoulder shaping
Bind off 8 (8, 9, 11, 11) sts at beg of next 2 rows, 8 (9, 10, 10, 11) sts at beg of next 4 rows. Sl rem 25 (27, 27, 27, 29) sts to a holder for back neck.

FRONT
Work as for back until piece measures 24 (24½, 25, 25½, 26)"/61 (62, 63.5, 65, 66)cm from beg.

Neck shaping
Next row (RS) K31 (33, 36, 38, 40) sts, join 2nd ball of yarn and bind off center 11 (13, 13, 13, 15) sts, k to end. Cont to work both sides at once binding off 3 sts from each neck edge once, 2 sts once and 1 st twice, AT SAME TIME, when

same length as back to shoulder, shape shoulder as on back.

SLEEVES
Cast on 37 (39, 39, 41, 41) sts.

Beg chart pat
Row 1 (RS) Beg with st 3 (2, 2, 1, 1), work row 1 of chart pat to st 39 (40, 40, 41, 41). Cont to foll chart in this way through row 60, then rep rows 39 to 49 once then cont in St st only, AT SAME TIME, inc 1 st each side every 4th row 9 (9, 11, 11, 13) times, every 6th row 8 (8, 7, 7, 6) times—71 (73, 75, 77, 79) sts. Work even until piece measures 21"/53cm from beg. Bind off.

FINISHING
Block pieces to measurements. Sew shoulder seams. Place marker at 10 (10½, 10¾, 11, 11¼)"/25.5 (26.5, 27, 28, 28.5)cm down from shoulder. Sew sleeves to armholes between markers. Sew side and sleeve seams.

Turtleneck
With circular needle, pick up and k 66 (72, 72, 72, 78) sts evenly around neck edge. Join and work in k3, p3 rib for 6½"/16.5cm. Bind off in rib.

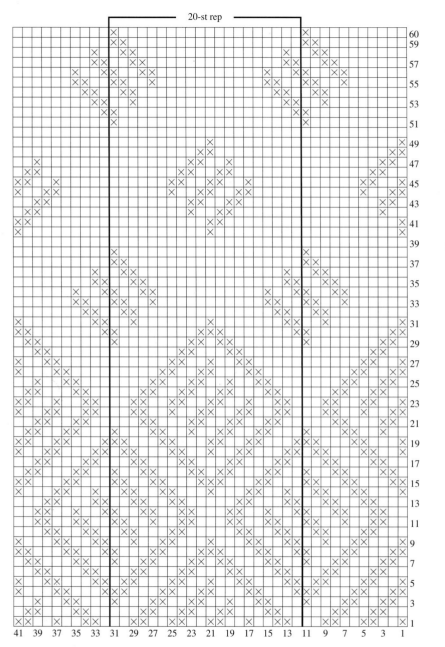

20-st rep

60, 59, 57, 55, 53, 51, 49, 47, 45, 43, 41, 39, 37, 35, 33, 31, 29, 27, 25, 23, 21, 19, 17, 15, 13, 11, 9, 7, 5, 3, 1

41 39 37 35 33 31 29 27 25 23 21 19 17 15 13 11 9 7 5 3 1

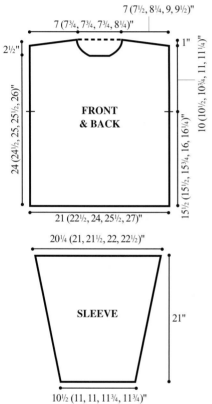

7 (7½, 8¼, 9, 9½)"

7 (7¾, 7¾, 7¾, 8¼)"

2½"

1"

10 (10½, 10¾, 11, 11¼)"

FRONT & BACK

24 (24½, 25, 25½, 26)"

15½ (15½, 15¾, 16, 16¼)"

21 (22½, 24, 25½, 27)"

20¼ (21, 21½, 22, 22½)"

SLEEVE

21"

10½ (11, 11, 11¾, 11¾)"

Stitch Key

☐ K on RS, p on WS

☒ P on RS, k on WS

Girl's Cropped Top & Cardigan

Designer Veronica Manno's carefree set is perfect for girls who just want to have fun. The tummy-baring top has elastic edges and button straps; toss on the matching short-sleeved cardigan or wear it on it's own. Both shown in size 4. The Girl's Cropped Top & Cardigan first appeared in the special Kids '01 issue of *Vogue Knitting*.

Girl's Cropped Top & Cardigan

VERY EASY VERY VOGUE

SIZES
To fit 4 (6, 8).

KNITTED MEASUREMENTS
Tube Top
● Chest 22½ (23½, 24½)"/57 (59.5, 62)cm
● Length 8 (9½, 10½)"/20.5 (24, 26.5)cm
Cardigan
● Chest 27 (29, 31)"/68.5 (73.5, 78.5)cm
● Length 11½ (12½, 14½)"/29 (32, 37)cm
● Upper arm 10 (11, 12)"/25.5 (28, 30.5)cm

MATERIALS
Tube Top
● 1 (1, 2) 1¾oz/50g balls (each approx 120yd/110m) of Filatura Di Crosa/Tahki•Stacy Charles, Inc. Brilla (rayon/cotton 3) in #381 hot pink (MC)
● 1 ball in #307 orange (CC)
● 2 cards of K1C2, LLC Rainbow Elastic size 1mm in #56 hot pink (MC)
● 1 card in #11 orange (CC)
● Size 4 (3.5mm) circular needle 24"/60cm long OR SIZE TO OBTAIN GAUGE
● Two ¾"/20mm flower buttons
● Stitch markers
Cardigan
● 2 (3, 3) 1¾oz/50g balls (each approx 120yd/110m) of Filatura Di Crosa/Tahki•Stacy Charles, Inc. Brilla (rayon/cotton 3) in #381 hot pink (MC)
● 1 ball in #307 orange (CC)
● One pair each sizes 4 and 5 (3.5 and 3.75mm) needles OR SIZE TO OBTAIN GAUGE
● Four ¾"/20mm flower buttons

TUBE TOP

GAUGE
24 sts and 32 rows/rnds = 4"/10cm over St st using size 4 (3.5mm) needles.
FOR PERFECT FIT, TAKE TIME TO CHECK GAUGE.

TOP
Beg at lower edge with 1 strand MC and matching elastic held tog, cast on 136 (140, 148) sts. Join to work in rnds. Pm at beg of rnd. Work in k2, p2 rib for 6 rnds, inc 0 (2, 0) sts on last rnd—136 (142, 148) sts. Work in St st until piece measures 4 (5, 6)"/10 (12.5, 15)cm from beg. Change to 1 strand CC and matching elastic and work in k2, p2 rib for 6 rnds. Bind off.

Straps
(make 2)
With MC, cast on 50 (58, 62) sts. Work in k2, p2 rib for 5 rows. Bind off.

FINISHING
Leaving 4"/10cm at center back free, sew on straps to inside of back for 1"/2.5cm. Leaving 4½ (5, 5½)"/11.5 (12.5, 14)cm at center front free, sew straps to front in same way. Sew button to center front rib at strap placement.

CARDIGAN

GAUGE
24 sts and 28 rows = 4"/10cm over St st using larger needles.
TAKE TIME TO CHECK GAUGE

BACK
With smaller needles and CC, cast on 82 (86, 90) sts. Work in k2, p2 rib for 6 rows inc 0 (0, 2) sts on last WS row—82 (86, 92) sts. Change to larger needles and MC and cont in St st until piece measures 11½ (12½, 14½)"/29 (32, 37)cm from beg. Bind off.

LEFT FRONT
With smaller needles and CC, cast on 34 (36, 38) sts. Work in k2, p2 rib for 6 rows. Change to larger needles and MC and cont in St st until piece measures 8½ (9½, 11½)"/21.5 (24.5, 29.5)cm from beg.

Neck shaping
Next row (WS) Bind off 5 sts, work to end. Cont to shape neck binding off 3 sts from neck edge once, 2 sts once. When same length as back, bind off 24 (26, 28) sts for shoulders.

RIGHT FRONT
Work as for left front reversing neck shaping.

SLEEVES
Sew shoulder seams. Pm at 5 (5½, 6)"/12.5 (14, 15)cm down from shoulders. With larger needles and MC, pick up and k 62 (66, 72) sts between markers along armhole edges. Work in St st for 3"/7.5cm. Change to smaller needles and CC. Work in k2, p2 rib for 6 rows. Bind off.

FINISHING
Block to measurements. Sew side and sleeve seams.

Button band

With smaller needles and CC, pick up and k 60 (66, 80) sts along left front edge. Work in k2, p2 rib for 6 rows. Bind off. Pm for 3 buttons on band, the first one at 1½"/4cm from neck edge and the others at 2"/5cm intervals. Work button-hole band along right front to corre-spond, binding off 2 sts for each button-hole on 3rd row and casting on 2 sts on foll row.

Neckband

With smaller needles and CC, pick up and k 66 (66, 70) sts evenly around neck edge. Work in k2, p2 rib for 6 rows, forming one more buttonhole in center of band to correspond to others. Sew on buttons.

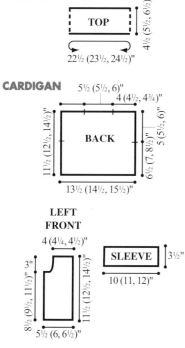

TUBE TOP

TOP

4½ (5½, 6½)"

22½ (23½, 24½)"

CARDIGAN

5½ (5½, 6)"

4 (4½, 4¾)"

BACK

11½ (12½, 14½)"

5 (5½, 6)"

6½ (7, 8½)"

13½ (14½, 15½)"

LEFT FRONT

4 (4¼, 4½)"

3"

8½ (9½, 11½)"

11½ (12½, 14½)"

5½ (6, 6½)"

SLEEVE

3½"

10 (11, 12)"

Resources

Write to the yarn companies listed below for yarn purchasing and mail-order information.
Resource information is current at time of publication.

ANNY BLATT
7796 Boardwalk
Brighton, MI 48116

BERROCO, INC.
PO Box 367
14 Elmdale Road
Uxbridge, MA 01569

BAABAJOES WOOL COMPANY
PO Box 260604
Lakewood, CO 80226

BROWN SHEEP CO.
100662 County Road 16
Mitchell, NE 69357

CLASSIC ELITE YARNS
300A Jackson Street, #5
Lowell, MA 01852

CLECKHEATON
distributed by
Plymouth Yarns

COLINETTE YARNS
distributed by
Unique Kolours

DI VÉ
distributed by
Lane Borgosesia

FILATURA DI CROSA
distributed by
Tahki•Stacy Charles, Inc.

GGH
distributed by
Muench Yarns

JAEGER HANDKNITS
5 Northern Blvd.
Amherst, NH 03031

JCA
35 Scales Lane
Townsend, MA 01469

K1C2, LLC
2220 Eastman Ave, #105
Ventura, CA 93003

KARABELLA YARNS, INC.
1201 Broadway Suite 311
New York, NY 10001

KOIGU WOOL DESIGNS
RR #1
Williamsford, ON N0H 2V0
Canada

LANE BORGOSESIA U.S.A.
PO Box 217
Colorado Springs, CO 80903

LION BRAND YARNS
34 West 15th Street
New York, NY 10011

MISSION FALLS
distributed by
Unique Kolours

MOKUBA
55 West 39 St.
New York, NY 10018
Canada: 577 Queen St. West
Toronto, ON MfV2B6

MUENCH YARNS
285 Bel Marin Keys Blvd. Unit J
Novato, CA 94949

NATURALLY
distributed by
S. R. Kertzer, Ltd.

ORNAGHI FILATI
distributed by
Trendsetter Yarns

PATON®
PO Box 40
Listowel, ON N4W 3H3
Canada

PLYMOUTH YARN
PO Box 28
Bristol, PA 19007

REYNOLDS
distributed by
JCA

ROWAN
5 Northern Blvd.
Amherst, NH 03031
UK: Green Lane Mill
Holmfirth
West Yorkshire HD7 1RW

SCHULANA
distributed by
Skacel Collection

SILK CITY
155 Oxford
Paterson, NJ 07522

SKACEL COLLECTION
PO Box 88110
Seattle, WA 98138
UK: Spring Mill House
Baildon, Shipley
West Yorkshire BD17 6AD

S.R. KERTZER, LTD.
105A Winges Road
Woodbridge, ON L4L 6C2
Canada

TAHKI YARNS
distributed by
Tahki•Stacy Charles, Inc.

TAHKI•STACY CHARLES, INC.
8000 Cooper Ave., Bldg. 1
Glendale, NY 11385

TRENDSETTER YARNS
16742 Stagg St., Suite 104
Van Nuys, CA 91406

UNIQUE KOLOURS
1428 Oak Lane
Downingtown, PA 19335

WOOL PAK YARNS NZ
distributed by
Baabajoes Wool Company

Vogue Knitting
233 Spring St.
New York, NY 10013-1252
Fax 646-336-3960
www.vogueknitting.com

We have made every effort to ensure the accuracy of the contents of this publication. We are not responsible for any human or typographical errors.

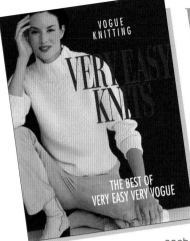
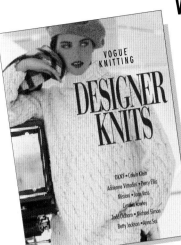

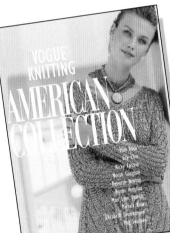

ACKNOWLEDGEMENTS

There were many people who contributed to the making of this book. In particular, and most importantly, we would like to thank all the past and present editors of *Vogue® Knitting* for their vision, inspiration and impeccable design selection. We would also like to extend our warmest gratitude to all of the designers, knitters, and technical experts whose skills and creative talents have enabled to bring the best of knitting to our readers and without whom the magazine would not be possible.

PHOTO CREDITS

Andrea Alberts (page 53), Paul Amato (pages 2, 11, 13, 15, 17, 19, 21, 23, 45, 46, 47, 49, 53, 58, 73, 81, 87, 89, 91, 107, 111, 113, 123, 129, 153, 160), Jeffrey Barone (pages 10, 35), Matthew Atanian (pages 141, 143), Carlo Dalla Chiesa (pages 67, 83), Bob Hiestra (page 75), Greg Hinsdale (pages 51, 97), Dan Howell (pages 133, 139, 148, 149), Nancy Levine (page 71), Barry McKinley (page 145), Francis Milon (pages 27, 29), Rudy Molacek (pages 65, 77, 79, 85), Dick Nystrom (pages 5, 103, 117, 125, 137, 147), Bruce Plotkin (pages 148, 155, 157), Peggy Sirota (pages 121, 127, 134, 135, 151), Albert Tolot (page 131), Robert Trachtenberg (page 33), Tom Wool (pages 25, 31, 37, 39, 41, 51, 55, 61, 95, 96, 101, 119).